THE JOSSEY-BASS ACADEMIC ADMINISTRATOR'S GUIDE TO

Hiring

The Jossey-Bass Academic Administrator's Guides are designed to help new and experienced campus professionals when a promotion or move brings on new responsibilities, new tasks, and new situations. Each book focuses on a single topic, exploring its application to the higher education setting. These real-world guides provide advice about day-to-day responsibilities as well as an orientation to the organizational environment of campus administration. From department chairs to office staff supervisors, these concise resources will help college and university administrators understand and overcome obstacles to success.

We hope you will find this volume useful in your work. To that end, we welcome your reaction to this volume and to the series in general, including suggestions for future topics.

THE JOSSEY-BASS

ACADEMIC ADMINISTRATOR'S
GUIDE TO

Hiring

JOSEPH G. ROSSE

ROBERT A. LEVIN

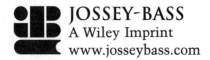

JOSSEY-BASS
A Wiley Imprint
www.josseybass.com

Published by Jossey-Bass
A Wiley Imprint
989 Market Street, San Francisco, CA 94103-1741   www.josseybass.com

This publication is designed to provide accurate and authoritative information in regard to the
subject matter covered. It is sold with the understanding that the author and publisher are not
engaged in rendering legal, accounting, or other professional service. If legal advice or other expert
assistance is required, the services of a competent professional person should be sought.

Jossey-Bass books and products are available through most bookstores. To contact Jossey-Bass
directly call our Customer Care Department within the U.S. at 800-956-7739, outside the U.S.
at 317-572-3986 or fax 317-572-4002.

Jossey-Bass also publishes its books in a variety of electronic formats. Some content that appears in
print may not be available in electronic books.

Library of Congress Cataloging-in-Publication Data

Rosse, Joseph G.
    The Jossey-Bass academic administrator's guide to hiring / Joseph G. Rosse, Robert A. Levin. —
1st ed.
        p.   cm.
Includes bibliographical references (p.   ) and index.
    ISBN 0-7879-6063-2 (alk. paper)
    1. Universities and colleges—Employees—Selection and appointment—United States.
2. College personnel management—United States. I. Levin, Robert A., 1957–   II. Title.
    LB2331.67.S44 R67 2003
    378.1'1—dc21

                                                                                    2002014343

Printed in the United States of America

FIRST EDITION

PB Printing 10   9   8   7   6   5   4   3   2   1

To our own teachers in higher education, with appreciation that they were hired and taught us, including:

Steve Arch, Will Bloch, Frank Gwilliam, Susan Hagmeier, Chuck Hulin, Loretta Morris, Christine Mueller, Greg Oldham, Rao Potluri, Ed Segel, and Leland Swenson.

—JGR and RAL

CONTENTS

PREFACE

THIS BOOK is intended to help people who work in higher education hire effectively. You, and other readers, may be involved in hiring in a variety of roles, as well as for different kinds of positions. As a department head, for example, you may be engaged in hiring an administrative assistant for the department office, three faculty members (perhaps two junior and one senior), and a new provost for the university. As a researcher, you may be involved in selecting technicians and postdocs for your lab. If you are a full-time administrator or staff supervisor, you could be involved in hiring for a range of positions from part-time custodial staff to computer programmers to administrative support to administrative colleagues.

Hiring for these different positions and in the various roles you have presents a number of challenges. In this book, we provide a common starting point for all of these challenges, a *performance foundation* that you can use for these and other hiring situations. The performance foundation allows you to connect hiring, retention, performance development, and performance assessment of any position through a common reference to performance: performance of the institution, performance of your unit, and performance of individuals in the job for which you are hiring.

It may seem obvious that there are different demands when hiring faculty, administrators, and staff. But take a moment to reflect on the causes of problems among the administrative and faculty hires you know about. If your experience in academia is at all like ours, you'll recognize that many fundamentals of both good and problem performance are common from position to position. Our approach is that the *processes* for developing a performance foundation, gathering information about applicants, and making hiring decisions are quite similar across positions and subject to many of the same hazards and solutions. Where we thought it helpful to note particular approaches to hiring faculty, administrators, or staff, we have done so.

Hiring "failures," whether in higher education or in business, is inherent in the difficult process of analyzing job requirements and applicant characteristics and then trying to make successful matches. Research shows that hiring mismatches cannot be eliminated, but it can be reduced to a level that creates fewer costs for institutions, for those with hiring responsibility, and for candidates—both those who are hired and those who are not. There is also a tremendous upside to making good matches when hiring in higher education. Because so many hires in higher education stay for a long period, either by design or happenstance, you can have a great impact on teaching, scholarship, and research by increasing the quality of the hires you make.

This book is designed from the ground up to help you do that. It is based on our earlier book, *High-Impact Hiring: A Comprehensive Guide to Performance-Based Hiring* (Jossey-Bass, 1997). We wrote that book for managers in business who have little training in the management of human resources and who find themselves frustrated with the challenges of hiring. In this book we have applied both the research and the practical solutions developed for *High-Impact Hiring* to the issues faced by those who make hiring decisions in higher education settings, and supplemented with new material specific to hiring in higher education. Our goal in both books is to help readers benefit from research-based and field-tested practices that can increase the effectiveness and efficiency of their hiring while also reducing frustration for the hiring decision maker.

The approach in this book can be distinguished by four primary characteristics:

> *Research-based.* How can you be confident that the information you learn in this book will actually increase the effectiveness of your hiring? Although both of the authors have had substantial

experience in developing selection systems, training managers in their use, and teaching courses on employee hiring and retention, we don't believe this experience can be equated by itself with effectiveness. Equally important is that the material in this book brings together years of empirical research, theoretical development, and field testing by a range of work scientists, including the authors. It is that accumulated knowledge base that provides the foundation for this book.

Understandable. If there is such extensive research on hiring, why is it that so many hiring decision makers continue to use seat-of-the-pants or "ritual" approaches to hiring? In large part it is because too little research has been translated into practical guidance. Moreover, much of the research has been conducted in and for organizations where centralized personnel specialists regularly hire hundreds or thousands of employees every year. The relevance of much of that research for academic administrators, who may make only a few hires per year, is not always readily apparent. Our goal is to adapt this rich research literature to suit *your* needs, whether you are a new department chair organizing your first faculty search, a senior administrator preparing to hire your university's first new provost in ten years, a manager who faces the ongoing challenge of hiring dozens of new staff every year, or a faculty member asked to chair or serve on a search committee.

Comprehensive. There is no one ideal hiring tool, nor is job performance unidimensional. As a result, hiring systems need to be comprehensive and robust, both in the attributes assessed and in the tools the systems use to guide hiring decisions. Our approach is based on the premise that an *integrated* set of selection procedures is the most effective way to *validly* assess the multiple attributes critical for success at most jobs.

Higher education focus. Higher education institutions face a set of challenges largely different from those faced by other employers. Although the similarities are probably increasing, the nature of much of the work, the source of funding, and many aspects of organizational culture remain different in academia. We have considered these differences in developing an approach to hiring that can build on the broad base of research developed outside of higher education and include solutions for situations unique to higher education.

We also note that much of our approach will be useful in academic institutions located in many parts of the world. For simplicity, we have used nomenclature common in U.S. universities. For example, we refer to *faculty* and *staff*, as is common in the United States, rather than to *academic staff* and *assistant staff*, as is common in British institutions. Our discussion of legal principles uses U.S. examples and is written primarily to a U.S. reader, but the emphasis on performance over law will be common to many institutional and legal systems.

PLAN OF THE BOOK

In Chapter One we describe the importance of effective hiring, the special challenges faced when hiring in higher education, and the three principles underlying our approach to hiring: performance orientation, systematic information gathering, and practical, systematic decision making. These principles, and the philosophy that underlies them, form the foundation for the rest of the book.

In Chapter Two we begin the process of creating an effective search. You'll learn tips about assembling and managing search committees and determining exactly what kind of candidate you need to hire. This is much more than filling out a job description or requisition. In Chapter Two we cover issues such as how to identify your organizational goals and then determine how these overarching goals form the performance objectives for the new hire. This performance foundation then becomes the basis for determining the knowledge, skills, and abilities you want to identify in applicants.

In Chapter Three we build on this base to determine how to attract applicants who possess these critical attributes. A key axiom is that the quality of the applicant pool places a cap on the quality of the individual you hire. In Chapter Three we describe procedures for attracting a pool of qualified applicants who are interested in your institution.

In Chapter Four we present a succinct, practical guide to some of the key legal issues that affect hiring decisions. The chapter is not designed to replace the advice of legal counsel but rather to alert you to issues so that you can hire in ways that prevent problems and to help you understand the basis for requirements or questions raised by legal counsel.

In Chapter Five we describe the process of gathering information to use in assessing applicants. Employers often take a narrowed approach to assessing applicants' qualifications, often relying almost exclusively on interviews. In this chapter, you will see how a tool, the *Performance Attributes Matrix,* can help you get the most information from vitae, interviews, work samples, and references, as well as other assessment procedures that have proven their value in other settings. In Chapter Five, you will also get researched-based practices and practical tips on effective interviewing, testing, and reference checking.

If you follow the recommendations in Chapters One through Five, you will have amassed a considerable amount of relevant information about each of your finalists. The next challenge is to determine how to combine this information to make a good decision. Research and experience demonstrate that this process presents demands that exceed the capabilities of the informal decision process used in most hiring decisions. In Chapter Six we introduce you to some practical, research-based approaches to making the decision process easier and more effective.

Hiring the right employee is only the first step toward making that person a critical component of your team. In the Afterword, you'll learn more about how to make sure the person you hire is able to fully contribute as quickly as possible, and also how to increase the likelihood that he or she will stay with your institution in an effective role.

Whether you are reading this book to prepare for your first hire or your fiftieth, you will be able to glean information and tips that make your job easier and your hiring more productive. As you read the material that follows and work to apply it in your institution, we hope that you will become as enthusiastic as we are about the potential of performance-based hiring systems to enhance the effectiveness of higher education.

ACKNOWLEDGMENTS

This approach to hiring for higher education draws on many years of work on hiring and performance, and each of our involvement in different ways with higher education. Over the years, we have discussed different aspects of hiring and performance in higher education with a number of colleagues in and out of the academy, in ways that were of benefit in preparing this book, including Maureen Ambrose, Susan Avery, David Balkin, Anne Bekoff, Alan Blackwell, Leslie Bohm, Rick Borkovec, Richard Byyny, Steve Dubovsky, Garth Eliason, Joe Falke, Bob Gatewood, David Grant, Steve Harris, Chuck Hulin, Richard Katz, Paula Liang, Ric Porreca, James F. Williams II, Chris Zafiratos, and Mike Zickar. Bill Hicks originally encouraged us to create a book with a research-based approach to hiring for performance, and we owed much at that time to the efforts of Susan Williams and Julianna Gustafson. We appreciate the encouragement and support of David Brightman and the Higher and Adult Education editorial and production team at Jossey-Bass / Wiley in extending that work to the higher education community.

Joseph Rosse
Robert Levin
Boulder, Colorado
August 2002

ABOUT THE AUTHORS

JOSEPH ROSSE and Robert Levin have worked together on hiring, retention, and work performance issues in organizations, including institutions of higher education, for more than a dozen years. Along with coauthoring journal articles and conference papers, they are the coauthors of *High-Impact Hiring: A Comprehensive Guide to Performance-Based Hiring* (Jossey-Bass, 1997) and *Talent Flow: A Strategic Approach to Keeping Good Employees, Helping Them Grow, and Letting Them Go* (Jossey-Bass, 2001). They recently cofounded the multidisciplinary Center for the Integrative Study of Work at the University of Colorado at Boulder. Earlier, they helped to cofound a multi-institutional research group looking at short-term and long-term performance issues in medical schools.

JOSEPH ROSSE is professor of management at the University of Colorado at Boulder (CU-Boulder), where he is also director and fellow of the Center for the Integrative Study of Work. He is chair of CU-Boulder's Human Research Committee and has served on numerous other committees, including the campus Administrator Appraisal Committee. He has served at CU-Boulder as faculty associate to the Vice Chancellor for Research and as IBM professor-in-residence. He has authored numerous research articles and book chapters on employee satisfaction and dissatisfaction, adaptive behavior, and employee selection. He holds a Ph.D. (1983) from the University of Illinois in industrial and organizational psychology. He is a member of the Society for Industrial and Organizational Psychology and the American Psychological Society.

ROBERT LEVIN is director and fellow of the Center for the Integrative Study of Work at the University of Colorado at Boulder. In 1986, he founded a private-sector work performance research organization, WorkScience/The Center for Human Function and Work, which is located at the University of Colorado at Boulder Research Park. He is chair of CU-Boulder's East Campus Research Association, has served as a lecturer in management at CU-Boulder, and most recently was a visiting research fellow in biological sciences at the University of Cambridge, conducting research on biological and psychological aspects of work performance. He holds a B.A. (1979) in biology from Reed College. He is a member of the American Association for the Advancement of Science and the American Psychological Society.

THE JOSSEY-BASS ACADEMIC ADMINISTRATOR'S GUIDE TO

Hiring

PART I

Introduction

1

The Challenge of Hiring in Higher Education

IGHER EDUCATION has been singularly successful at convincing our constituents that education is the engine of both individual and societal success. The support provided to institutions of higher education for research and teaching is based on an implied contract with society as a whole and with legislative bodies, granting agencies, and donors for extremely high-quality outcomes. Far more than in most organizations, the quality of these outcomes depends on the quality of the people who are hired and retained. Faculty, whether in the classroom or in the laboratory, provide the inspiration, creativity, and dedication that are the heart and soul of colleges and universities. Staff provide the support to both faculty and students that often makes the difference between excellence and mediocrity. And administrators can provide the vision, direction, and resources to make the work of faculty, staff, and students possible.

Yet as you probably already know from your own experience—whether hiring or being hired—conducting hiring in higher education involves some special challenges. Colleges and universities often have complex and sometimes bureaucratic procedures for hiring compared with hiring in many business enterprises. Moreover, many jobs in higher education are highly specific; whereas a private business may be able to hire a salesperson with pharmaceutical experience to sell air conditioners, it's impossible to hire an experienced sociologist for a molecular biology position. And it's often more difficult to correct hiring errors in a higher education institution. Make no mistake, private enterprises accumulate deadwood, and people do move from one institution to another in higher education. But in many schools, hiring and firing of staff is based on a civil service system, a tenure system, or procedures set by a governing board, so it's fair to assume that hiring decisions, once made, cannot be unmade lightly.

At the same time, hiring in higher education has certain advantages over hiring in private industry. When hiring faculty and administrators, decision makers have access to a verifiable record of research and administrative achievements that is simply not available for virtually any private sector hire. Well-enshrined hiring procedures, such as use of search committees and job talks, help reduce impulsive hiring decisions. Moreover, the culture of rigor and quality that exists in most higher education settings creates a climate conducive to hiring top-quality candidates. But as with most things in life, the devil is in the details of putting these theoretical advantages to work for you. If it's your job to read through vitae for thirty candidates, or if the search committee you are participating in or chairing either has its mind made up or too many issues about which to bicker and fight, you might appreciate the quality obtainable from the process in theory but regret its application in practice.

This book is intended to help you make high-quality hires in three fundamental ways. First, the foundation of our approach to hiring, whether in higher education or in the private sector, is grounded in performance. We want to provide you with ways to identify the most important aspects of performance and then develop effective ways to match these essential aspects of performance with candidates' abilities and skills.

Second, our approach to gathering reliable information about performance and using this information to make valid decisions about hiring is based on research, which we present here in practical application. Research in psychology and decision making, as well as years of applied research in many areas, can provide guidance on what information to gather, how to gather it (and not gather it), and how to use it in making hiring decisions that can make substantial differences in the proportion of good hiring decisions you and your colleagues make.

Third, our approach is intended to help you navigate some of the unique aspects of hiring in higher education. An academic vita, for example, contains far more information than most business résumés. How can you make use of that information effectively, and what pitfalls must you avoid? Search committees are also relatively unique to academia, and pose both opportunities and challenges for enhancing the success of hiring. Yet job interviews in academia and in industry are more similar than they are different. The interviews you conduct can benefit from accumulated research and practice on effective and ineffective interviewing, so you can change the interview process from one of the least valid predictors of performance to one of the most valid.

A FRAMEWORK FOR PERFORMANCE-BASED HIRING

Academics are accustomed to thinking about theories, models, and frameworks, so we hope that readers will be encouraged to know that the principles and practices described in this book are grounded in nearly a century's worth of theory and empirical research, as well as practical experience. What we describe are neither random observations, personal opinions, nor cookbook approaches to hiring. Rather, our approach is based on three fundamental principles that form a framework for effective hiring:

- Performance orientation

- Systematic information gathering

- Rational, realistic decision making

Performance Orientation
The most fundamental principle underlying effective hiring is performance orientation. This principle recognizes that organizations, including educational institutions, exist to perform work toward a purpose.

Every organizational decision should be based on contribution to performance, and hiring is no exception.

Consider, for example, a decision to make a major purchase of computer systems for a new instructional lab. Computers and their associated software can be purchased for many purposes from word-processing to e-mail and Web access to high-speed numerical computations. The way computers are configured can make them more or less effective for the various possible uses, so an effective purchase decision needs to be based on an analysis of intended uses. Whether the cases for the computers are ivory, matte black, or neon blue is not a performance-relevant factor, even though you may have a personal penchant for raspberry red. Having a flat-panel display or the latest and fastest processor may or may not be performance-relevant, even though both may have prestige value when showing off the new lab to alumni or potential students.

Simply knowing that you need fifty new computers for a new lab is not enough. You need to know for what purposes those computers will be used, both now and during their effective lifetime. Only then can you determine memory and processor requirements, what type of software should be bundled with them, and whether you need laptop computers or desktop units.

We're not suggesting that candidates for assistant professor or administrative assistant can be configured like computers. What is critical about the analogy is the importance of understanding and deciding about performance needs *before* ever beginning to evaluate which candidates might fit those needs.

In the next chapter you will learn how to develop some practical performance objectives for your own work unit (whether that unit is your own lab, a department, or a larger academic unit) and then use this information to understand what performances you require from someone you hire. This approach will draw on your experience and will free you from relying on more typical ways of developing hiring standards, such as job descriptions that may be outdated or inaccurate. The result is a clearer picture of what you're looking for as you recruit and evaluate candidates. This avoids the equivalent of purchasing a supercomputer to send e-mail. It also avoids the common problem of arguing about candidates before deciding about priorities.

Performance orientation is a necessary but insufficient condition for effective hiring. To be successful, performance orientation must be carried out via systematic information gathering and then implemented through effective decisions.

Systematic Information Gathering

Organizational processes need to be systematic in order to be effective, and that applies as much to hiring as it does to other processes on campus. Researchers conducting clinical trials of a new drug don't just decide one day to increase dosages, add a new drug to subjects' regimens, or move half of the control group to a treatment arm. Nor do effective instructors decide one semester to drop part of their curriculum or change from lectures to case studies on a whim, any more than administrators schedule classes by simply telling all the faculty and students to show up for the first day of classes on September 1 and figure out when and where they will meet for the rest of the term.

Instead, these decisions are driven by systematic collection and analysis of reliable and relevant information. Effective hiring also depends upon reliable information. The first type of information concerns the nature of work that needs to be done to meet the goals of the program area. Vague, outdated, or misguided performance objectives make it difficult or impossible to conduct performance-focused hiring. The second type of information concerns characteristics of applicants. Effective hiring demands hiring tools that provide you with reliable, valid, job-related information about applicants' qualifications; we will have much to say about this in Chapter Five.

Rational, Realistic Decision Making

Making rational, realistic decisions about who to hire is the third fundamental principle of an effective hiring system. A *rational* decision process is based on the best information possible, gathered systematically. A *realistic* decision process acknowledges that even with the best information gathering, decisions have to be made with limited and incomplete information (Simon, 1976). Hiring decisions are probabilistic estimates of what particular individuals may do sometime in the future. As such, the outcomes of such decisions are even more uncertain than decisions about complex physical systems, such as the weather. In addition to being complex, human behavior is characterized by two factors that add complexity not seen in physical systems:

1. *Cognition and learning.* People can learn to do things in the future that they cannot do today. As a consequence, two people with similar knowledge, skills, or abilities may turn out to have much different levels of job performance at some arbitrary point in the future. And at some other point even further in the future, the rank ordering of these individuals may change once again. As a result, even correct information will more accurately predict an applicant's initial job performance than it will performance over a longer period (Hulin, Henry, & Noon, 1990).

2. *Choice and motivation.* A person may have excellent analytical and interpersonal skills, for example, but choose not to apply those skills with as much diligence as another individual with more modest skills and abilities. Or the person may decide to quit and apply those skills at another employer. In part these motivational patterns may be predictable from differences in disposition, but to a large extent they result from less predictable reactions to such work characteristics as the type of work, level of challenge, quality of supervision, support from coworkers, and amount and form of compensation (Levin & Rosse, 2001; Rosse & Hulin, 1985).

Humans' ability to change means that no matter how much you might want to, you cannot predict a candidate's future performance with the same precision that astronomers can predict solar eclipses. In fact, attempting to do so can lead to serious mistakes in decision making, and these mistakes are compounded in the long-term hires made in academic institutions. The methods we present for making hiring decisions are effective precisely because they recognize the future-oriented, probabilistic nature of hiring decisions.

HIRING APPROACHES TO AVOID

Many hiring processes pay lip service to performance, without tying all aspects of the hiring process closely to performance. There are many patterns of non-performance-based hiring that can be observed in private industry. We call one such pattern *warm-body hiring,* from a comment one manager made that he often found himself hiring "anyone with a warm body and the ability to pass a drug test." Although it might seem that this kind of hiring without regard to qualifications would not exist in higher education, one can occasionally see examples in which unit heads, frustrated by shortages of applicants with the qualities they would like, give up and engage in what one administrator referred to as "lottery hiring"—hiring almost randomly in the hopes of getting an occasional winner.

We have also seen warm-body hiring at work in faculty and administrator hires. One of our own doctoral students was invited to an on-site "interview" for a faculty position that lasted only two hours, including a fifteen-minute presentation of her research. She quite literally spent more time flying to and from the campus than she did interacting with her potential colleagues. We also recall a search for a senior administrative position that resulted in a dark horse candidate being offered the job with minimal vetting because of a stalemate over the front-runners. It should not be surprising that after a tumultuous few years this individual left the job, to the relief of many.

Generally, though, dysfunctional hiring patterns such as these are rare in higher education because of the long established traditions of hiring procedures. Yet these same traditions and procedures mean that higher education institutions are at least as prone to another kind of non-performance-based hiring, which we call *ritual hiring.* In ritual hiring, organizations or individuals continue to use well-worn procedures without evaluating whether the procedures predict performance—or actually favor lower-performing candidates. These non-performance-based hiring rituals can be far more insidious than warm-body hiring. When an employer conducts warm-body hiring, it knows it is not devoting the resources to effective selection and is more likely to proceed accordingly. But hiring rituals give everyone involved the warm illusion of thorough selection, even though the time and energy expended may in fact produce no better results than a warm-body approach—and at times, worse results.

What kinds of rituals are we talking about? As one example, extensive research demonstrates that the venerable unstructured selection interview predicts performance little better than chance; yet interviews can readily be structured around performance criteria to vastly increase their predictive power. The job talk for an academic position can be a highly predictive performance test or a predetermined ritual, depending on how it is structured and evaluated. Meetings of search committees and decision processes of selection committees are rituals that can frequently lead to the wrong candidate being chosen for the job for the wrong reasons. Despite their popularity, research shows that panel interviews often have much lower validity than individual interviews, although their validity can be greatly enhanced by managing how the group determines performance standards and asks questions.

Performance-based hiring is thus an antidote to ritual hiring. The first time you implement performance-based hiring, you can sweep away long-standing impediments to effective hiring and modify others to aid in predicting performance. As you continue to implement a performance-based approach, you can establish new practices and habits that help institutionalize an ongoing commitment to hiring for performance.

Every hire you make can have a substantive impact on the quality of higher education at your institution. A dean at a large research university once told us that his legacy to the quality of higher education twenty, thirty, and forty years from now resulted from the quality of hiring he did today. By using a hiring process grounded in performance, based on research, and built on effective practices, you can make sure that your hires continue to leave a positive legacy for future generations of students and scholars.

PART II

Getting Prepared

2

Preparing for Hiring

YOU'VE RECEIVED authorization and a budget line to proceed with a new hire, and you're committed to hiring in a systematic and performance-focused way. So where do you start? In this chapter you'll learn three early steps:

- Determining who will be involved in the hiring process

- Identifying what you are looking for in a job candidate

- Creating a compensation package for the position

THE CRITICAL ROLE OF SEARCH COMMITTEES

One of the most basic questions in hiring is who makes the hiring decision. In a few situations in higher education you may make the hiring decision individually, for instance as the direct supervisor of a staff position (probably with some consultation with the human resources department, as well as your colleagues). If so, it is still useful to read this section with an eye towards tasks or issues that must be attended to regardless of who is the final hiring authority. Most hiring in academic institutions, though, is coordinated by a search committee. Search committees are consistent with the egalitarian traditions of universities, particularly regarding faculty hiring.

Nonetheless, conducting hiring by search committee is no guarantee of a good outcome. In fact, some have suggested that many hiring mistakes can be traced back to ineffective search committee composition or process (Nelson, 1997). Research shows that involving more people in the hiring process often produces no improvement in the quality of hiring decisions (McDaniel, Whetzel, Schmidt, & Maurer, 1994). Hires done by search committees are more costly than those done by a single person because more person-hours of valuable effort will be expended in the process. Thinking carefully about how best to establish and run a search process so that beneficial results are maximized and problems with costs and hiring mistakes are minimized will be well worth your time.

Determining the Role of the Search Committee

The first requirement for an effective search is clarity about the search committee's charge. The chair of the committee should make it explicit to whom the committee reports and what the committee is being asked to do. Most search committees serve in an advisory capacity; the actual hiring decision is made by a dean, lab or center director, college president, or governing board. If so, it's important to clarify what degree of autonomy the committee has in determining performance qualifications and salary. It's also important to know whether the committee is charged with providing one or multiple candidates, whether multiple candidates are supposed to be rank-ordered, whether the hiring authority has to approve invitations for on-campus visits, and what the committee's options are when confronted with a less-than-desirable talent pool. It is also useful to clarify expectations regarding the timetable for the search and to determine what level of flexibility should be allowed for candidates who miss application deadlines (although one general rule is not to begin interviewing candidates until any stated deadline has passed, so that all timely applications receive a fair review). Failing to make these and related expectations explicit can be a source of considerable frustration down the road.

One administrator we know, charged with chairing a search committee for a highly visible position and asked to do so after a first search had failed, gathered his search committee together for their first meeting and made a speech that went about like this: "We are a search committee, not a selection committee. Our job is to generate high-quality candidates, learn about them, sort through them, and recommend a number of finalists to the president, who will make the selection decision. We do not make selection decisions here, and I won't stand for you advocating, including, or choosing a particular candidate you want to be chosen."

At the other end of the continuum, some committees—particularly in independent research institutions—are given "full power" (a parliamentary term) to conduct the hire. If you are on a committee that has been given full power, avoid later misunderstandings by making sure that everyone who will be affected by the hire understands that the committee itself will be making the hiring decision.

Composition of the Search Committee

The first decision about the composition of a search committee deals with appointing a chair. For faculty searches, the chair of the committee is generally a tenured faculty member of rank greater or equal to the position being recruited. Administrators generally should not chair searches for faculty positions, since doing so may violate expectations regarding faculty governance and may also lead to the perception that they are directing the process toward a favored candidate. Moreover, since search committees are usually advisory, the final decision generally rests with the administrator. Department chairs and other midlevel administrators may be more likely to chair committees formed to hire senior staff (such as center or laboratory directors), and both administrators and faculty are often called on to participate in search committees for higher-level administrators.

Generally, the chair works with the final hiring authority to decide on the remaining members of the search committee. As much as possible, the search committee members should represent the key constituencies who will be affected by the employee to be hired, and should bring different perspectives about the position. Depending on the position, the search committee may include faculty, students, and staff within the unit, as well as faculty or staff from other units. For senior administrative positions, the committee may also involve the larger community, as represented by alumni or employers of students. At the same time, do not allow the committee to become so large that scheduling meetings becomes impossible or interaction is stifled. Keeping the committee membership between five and nine members will provide an effective balance between these concerns for most searches.

One of the temptations when creating a "representative" search committee (particularly those searching for senior administrators) is to add members whose positions make the committee look more impressive or credible but who will contribute little to the committee's work. The committee chair should resist this pressure vigorously. The work of the committee is too important to waste a slot on someone who doesn't contribute or, far worse, who waits until the final meetings to weigh in on candidates without the benefit of earlier discussion of hiring requirements.

According to faculty hiring expert Mike Nelson (Nelson, 1997), it's important to recognize that some faculty are not well suited to participate effectively in a search. He suggests that if committees are to hire the best applicants, they must comprise members who

- Are experts in the field in which the new hire will be working, because those who are thoroughly familiar with the literature are in the best position to identify superior candidates

- Welcome hiring superior performers, rather than feeling threatened by them

- Are willing and able to expend the considerable time required of a search committee

Whether or not you agree with Nelson's contention, it's useful to apply these criteria when thinking about whom to invite. For search committee members who might not be expected to be expert in a field, you could revise the first criterion to "willingness to become familiar with the duties the job entails." The second and third criteria are essential to conduct an effective search based on performance. After drafting an initial list of members, also consider the overall composition of the committee to ensure that all members will be comfortable sharing their ideas about both the process and the candidates.

Optimizing the Search Committee Process

A key challenge for any committee chair is to lead the committee's work in a way that maximizes the positive contributions of its members. Even a committee comprising exceptional individuals can produce poor outcomes if the group's work is not managed effectively. Groups have many potential advantages relative to individual decision makers, since they presumably bring a broader range of ideas, provide multiple perspectives on applicants' qualifications, and can engage in synergistic thinking that produces creative and effective solutions. On the flip side, they take more time (and far more person-hours of labor) to make a decision, provide no guarantee of making a better decision than any one individual, and can regress into a cesspool of bickering and dissension. The difference between these two outcomes has as much to do with how the committee does its business as who is on the committee (Guzzo & Dickson, 1996).

Agreeing on Outcomes First

If you take one nugget away from this chapter, we hope it is this: for any search committee to be effective, it's essential that long before considering any candidates, those involved in making the hire agree on the *outcomes* of the hire and the critical *attributes* that successful candidates should possess. This should occur *before* creating a position announcement, reviewing CVs, or interviewing candidates. Making good decisions about critical performance requirements will have the single greatest effect on the quality of your hire and on eliminating the squabbles that often accompany academic hiring (Highhouse & Johnson, 1996).

Moreover, getting a search committee, board, or administrative group to decide about outcomes and attributes fosters an effective group process. This is the time to air differing opinions about what the position should be for (the outcomes) and what kind of qualifications are needed (the attributes), involve various stakeholders, and make decisions, even when consensus agreements can't be reached. Hence, if the math department has a new faculty line, take the time early in the process and long before considering individual candidates to hash out whether a number theorist or a mathematical statistician should be hired and whether she or he will be hired primarily based on capabilities for research, graduate advising, undergraduate teaching, outreach to business and industry, or some combination of these.

We recall an example at a highly-regarded research institution where a search was under way for a tenured hire that could free up a senior researcher for new pursuits. The committee never decided whether the hire should be a close match with the senior researcher's area or contribute more generally to the breadth of the department. As a result, the two finalists represented one candidate from each "camp," and the hiring decision was reduced to an argument over which approach should prevail. Imagine how this went over for the finalist who "lost." He was told that he was actually more highly qualified than the successful candidate, but the committee had decided to go with the other area of strength. This reflects badly on the institution, on the successful candidate, and on the quality of the search.

To emphasize the importance of the committee's decisions about outcomes and attributes, and to put some teeth into them, it's a good practice to get the committee to agree at the outset that evaluations of candidates will be performed only by those committee members who first participate in determining the desired outcomes of the hire and the critical attributes desired of candidates.

Essential Role of the Search Committee Chair

The search committee chair plays a critical role in guiding the committee's work. At the most basic level, the chair provides structure to the search process by developing and following an overall hiring plan and creating a timetable for critical checkpoints.

The chair can also optimize efficiency by dividing the work among members in a way that effectively uses each member's talents. For example, the chair might begin by identifying a person who is responsible for filing and tracking applicants' material and taking care of routine correspondence with applicants. A careful and complete record of correspondence should be maintained; keeping a checklist of necessary material to be received or sent in each applicant's file can be a useful way to keep track of what needs to be done (Waggaman, 1983). Check with your institution's human resources director to determine what materials should be retained at the end of the search, and for how long.

A next step might be to assign a subcommittee of appropriate members the task of prescreening incoming vitae. The chair might then delegate to others the responsibility to conduct reference checks, particularly if they know personally some of the reference providers. Another common strategy is to assign certain committee members to be hosts or coordinators for campus visits. Division of labor lightens the load on each committee member, especially the chair, who otherwise may be burdened with trying to do it all. When it comes to reviewing semifinalists and finalists, though, it is important that *all* committee members are intimately familiar with each candidate.

If a subcommittee is going to conduct prescreening of vitae or applications, it's important to define the subcommittee's role and power. In one approach, a subcommittee could be charged with screening in an advisory capacity only: all application files would be reviewed by the subcommittee and then returned to the committee with a summary report and recommendations for finalists, but all committee members could then review all dossiers in light of the recommendations. In a second approach, the subcommittee could instead be charged with reporting on finalists to the search committee as a whole. In this instance, the subcommittee would nominate finalists (and provide some description of the approach used for determining finalists), and the committee would then vote on whether to accept the subcommittee's report of that slate of finalists. A third approach would give the subcommittee full power to review the applicants and choose the finalists, on which the full committee would then proceed. Whatever the approach that fits your search best, make the charge for the subcommittee clear.

Finally, the search chair has the critical role of ensuring even-handed and thorough consideration of all candidates. The chair must be sure that all committee members are aware of, and comply with, appropriate legal, ethical, and performance bases for evaluating candidates. This even-handed thoroughness begins with the very first meeting, and culminates in ensuring a balanced discussion of finalists, untainted by bias or by pressure from powerful search committee members.

WHAT WILL A GOOD CANDIDATE LOOK LIKE?

The most critical step toward making an effective hiring decision is deciding exactly what it is that you are looking for in a new hire. As obvious as this may seem, it is a step that is often given short shrift. In such situations, job descriptions for hiring can be nonexistent or based on performance-irrelevant factors such as

- Job requirements that existed once but are now an anachronism. This is particularly a problem for technical positions or other jobs that experience rapid or repeated changes.

- A desire to "clone" oneself or the prior jobholder. People naturally enjoy being around people like themselves, so there is a tendency to describe job requirements in terms that we are used to and comfortable with. Although compatibility is important for many jobs, hiring similar individuals can produce an overly homogeneous work group and an imbalance of critical skills.

- A desire to hire someone who is just the opposite of the previous (usually unsuccessful) jobholder. Although there may be good reasons to avoid repeating a disastrous situation, focus on the necessary qualifications for improved performance rather than automatically reject anyone who appears similar to the past incumbent.

- A "silver bullet"—a particular attribute that is hoped to solve all a unit's problems. Common examples of silver-bullet attributes include charismatic leadership, fundraising prowess, or outstanding publication records. Although each of these may be important for certain jobs, focusing only on one attribute can easily lead to hiring a one-dimensional candidate with fatal flaws. The charismatic president may have a complete absence of fiscal responsibility, the dean who has excellent fundraising skills may fail to rally faculty around a college's mission, and the star researcher may be a dud in the classroom.

- The characteristics of the candidates themselves. Too often search committee members decide what they're looking for not as the first step in the search process but as they review the résumés of applicants (Murray, 1999). This tendency can be a particular problem when units decide to hire the "best" person available rather than deciding in advance what kind of employee would add the most value to their unit.

Instead of these potentially dysfunctional approaches to position descriptions, you want to develop a profile of the critical attributes necessary for effective performance and longevity in a job. This is the first step in a process that we refer to as *developing a performance foundation* that links the performance needs of your unit to the basis for hiring, developing, retaining, and evaluating the performance of people in your organization.

Developing a Performance Foundation

The success of a new hire depends on that person advancing the performance of his or her unit toward meeting the goals of the institution. The purpose of developing a performance foundation is to develop a shared understanding of how a particular job affects the success of an office, lab, or department and from that identify the profile of knowledge, skills, abilities, and other attributes (often referred to as KSAOs and described in more detail later in this chapter) that a job candidate must possess in order to contribute to successful unit performance.

Linking Hiring Requirements to Mission

Although institutions of higher education share much in common, it is important to think through the implications of differences in mission (Van der Vorm, 2001). By *mission* we mean the long-term aims, goals, and values of the institution as a whole and of your own unit. To take just one portion of institutional mission as an example, land-grant universities were formed to provide research and educational services to a state's citizens, often with a particular emphasis on the needs of agricultural community interests. Community colleges generally have a particularly strong teaching mission, serving a broad spectrum of students. Some private universities may have a mission to serve particular groups, such as women, those seeking a military education, or those of a particular religion. Other institutions may focus on research or technical leadership, either broadly or in particular domains. Each of these missions will have an effect on how successful performance is defined and on the qualifications needed for a new employee to be successful. A prolific researcher whose life revolves around a particular area of inquiry and who dislikes classroom teaching is not likely to be a good fit for schools whose forte is teaching, but such a person might be a good fit for a dedicated research position within a research institute or academic center.

In a similar fashion, units (colleges, departments, work groups) within an institution need to ask how they contribute to the mission of the institution. Some academic units may be identified as so-called "centers of research excellence" and play a disproportionate role in advancing the research mission of a university. Others may be nationally known for a particular program of study. Still others may serve the mission of the institution by providing courses that form the foundation for students' advanced studies or by providing services essential for research or administrative activities. When making a hire for a unit, the fundamental question that has to be answered is, What are the aims of this unit, consistent with the aims of the institution, that will be advanced by this hire and how?

Once you know what you want to accomplish as a unit, you can then ask what tasks each person has to accomplish, or what outcomes each person has to reach, to meet those unit-level objectives. Analyzing what it takes to accomplish these *tasks* or *outcomes* is the primary basis for identifying performance-related qualifications for a job.

You also want to identify job-relevant *Risk Factors*, which are behaviors or outcomes that are detrimental to the unit or organization mission, and *Fit Factors*, which are characteristics that are important for assuring that the new employee will be satisfied as well as productive in your particular situation. Risk Factors and Fit Factors will be described in more detail later in the chapter.

Identifying Critical Job Tasks or Outcomes
Traditionally, job descriptions have been based on an analysis of the critical *tasks* that a job incumbent performs. A task is a set of related activities directed toward a particular purpose. If you are the supervisor for the

position being hired you can probably create a list of critical tasks fairly quickly. If you are less familiar with the job, or if a search committee is involved, you might interview a few incumbents and the direct supervisor to help generate the list of tasks.

In some cases, theory or research can also be useful for identifying critical tasks. For example, Chickering and Gamson (1994) derived the following characteristics of effective college teaching from the research literature:

- Encouraging contact between students and instructor
- Developing reciprocity and cooperation among students
- Using active learning techniques
- Giving prompt feedback
- Emphasizing time on task
- Communicating high expectations
- Respecting diverse talents and ways of learning

Not all tasks are absolutely essential for most jobs, so the next step is to narrow your list of tasks to those that are essential or critical. As you will learn in Chapter Four, identifying essential duties of a job is also important for meeting legal obligations. One good way to do this is to have a small set of people who know the job well rate each of the tasks in terms of *frequency* of occurrence, *difficulty* of performing, and *criticality of outcome*. Criticality of outcome is an assessment of the seriousness of the consequences of not performing the task or of performing it inadequately. Only tasks with high ratings (for example, four on a one-to-five scale) should be considered essential; parsimony and logistics suggest that for most jobs there should be no more than six or eight essential tasks. An example of a critical task analysis is shown in Exhibit 2.1.

Distinguishing Between Certainty- and Uncertainty-Based Hiring

The task-based approach we just described has been criticized for being too static and for assuming that jobs exist in a vacuum (Sanchez, 1994; Carson & Stewart, 1995). Tasks change as demands evolve over time,

Exhibit 2.1. Critical Task Analysis for Residence Hall Advisor.

Task	Importance
Coordinates responses to crises	4.8
Monitors residence halls to maintain security	4.5
Enforces housing department rules and regulations	4.5
Assists in resolution of disputes	4.4
Counsels and advises students about personal or academic issues	4.2
Provides information to residents	4.0
Develops educational programs for residents	3.5

employees tailor jobs to fit their particular interests and strengths, and tasks are shared among a set of individuals (in team-based work, for example). The concern is that this dynamic quality of work makes it difficult or impossible to base hiring decisions on task-based job descriptions.

Our view is that there is some validity to these arguments, depending on the nature of the job for which you are hiring (Rosse & Levin, 1997). A traditional task-based approach—what we refer to as *certainty-based hiring*—is appropriate for jobs that are relatively stable during the typical tenure of an employee, for which performance expectations can be anticipated and described, and in which individuals work fairly autonomously. This characterization describes many jobs in higher education from faculty positions to many administrative jobs. We are not suggesting that these jobs do not, or should not, change. Rather, we are suggesting that for many jobs the changes are either relatively slow and predictable or turnover is frequent enough that the changes are not likely to dramatically affect the employees you are hiring at any one point during their time working at this job.

There are some jobs, however, for which this characterization does not hold, a situation we refer to as *uncertainty-based hiring*. For example, the roles of college presidents and deans have undergone considerable change over the last few decades, with greater emphasis on financial and managerial responsibilities and less on traditional "scholarly" activities

(Marcus, 2001; Wolverton, Gmelch, & Montez, 2001). Information technology (IT) specialists are an example of a higher education job that did not even exist a generation ago but that has become vitally important and increasingly dynamic. Other jobs may be conducted in a team- or project-based environment in which tasks may be divided up based on the changing composition of a team or the specific demands of different project assignments.

When conducting uncertainty-based hiring, it makes sense to focus on critical *outcomes* rather than, or in addition to, critical tasks. How outcomes are attained may vary according to who is in a team, what new technologies become available, or the demands of a new situation, but the *core* outcomes—and their relationship to the mission of the unit and institution—are likely to remain fairly stable. For example, the tasks required of an administrator charged with developing a university's new initiative in information technology may change over time, but the outcome of enhancing the quality of research, teaching, and service should stay largely the same. In all hires, and particularly with uncertainty-based hiring, you should also be thinking about what the essential outcomes or duties are likely to be in the foreseeable future, rather than focusing only on what is critical currently.

Certainty- and uncertainty-based hiring represent the poles of a continuum; in many cases it's worth thinking through which aspects of a position are certainty-based and which are uncertainty-based. For example, faculty are often hired to fill positions in new and emerging areas, and thus many of the factors will be uncertainty-based, and those aspects of the hire should focus on identifying critical outcomes. Even in these cases, however, there will be other aspects of the job that will be more certainty-based, and for these aspects, identifying critical tasks will help make an effective hire.

Identifying Risk Factors

So far you have focused on identifying tasks or outcomes that contribute to the success of your unit and institution. Although this provides the core of the performance foundation, it's important to remember—and easy to overlook—the behaviors or outcomes that can be detrimental.

Here we're talking about the dark side of performance, things we'd rather not think about but that can create major problems if ignored. One example that is important for many academic positions is sexual harassment. This is a behavior that is detrimental to all organizations but can be particularly pernicious in higher education because of the close contact between students and faculty or staff. Since incidents of harassment can be devastating to the target and harmful to morale and the reputation of the institution, it's important to consider applicants' history of sexual harassment for positions that provide a potential for it to occur. We also hasten to add that this is an example of a behavior that cannot be eliminated solely through hiring, so every institution needs to have strong policies and procedures for handling sexual harassment that may occur despite your best efforts in the hiring process. This is true for most other types of Risk Factors as well.

Another potentially relevant Risk Factor is dishonesty. For positions with access to money or other valuables, dishonesty might involve theft, embezzlement, or directing funds inappropriately to pet programs. In other cases, it may involve inappropriate access to privileged information, such as personal information about students, faculty, or staff. For faculty, it might involve academic integrity in the treatment of research data, plagiarism, or ethical treatment of students.

For some positions, safety may be a relevant Risk Factor. Maintenance workers, particularly more specialized employees working in physically risky environments such as campus powerhouses, boiler rooms, or laboratories, may pose a risk to themselves and others if they have a lackadaisical attitude toward safety. The same will be true for faculty and research workers in lab settings.

As important as it is to focus on superior job performance, you should not overlook factors that relate to unusual but costly anomalies. Even if infrequent, Risk Factors should be evaluated during the hiring process if their consequences are significant.

Identifying Fit Factors

Issues of "organizational fit" are controversial. The argument for considering fit is that looking only at the technical ability to perform a job ignores contextual factors that can affect both performance and longevity of a newly hired employee (Kaplowitz, 1986; Marchese & Lawrence, 1988). Moreover, working in higher education is different from working in other fields, even for jobs that might seem identical. Clerical and administrative employees used to working in a corporate setting, for example, may find the working climate in a public university to be more bureaucratic at the same time that it may be more intellectually charged.

Differences in organizational culture are apparent between private and publicly funded schools, between schools that place more emphasis on research or on teaching, between "commuter" schools and those with large residential populations, and so forth. Work climates may also vary substantially between units of a single institution because of differences in leader style, history, mission, and interaction patterns. These differences can have a substantial effect on whether an otherwise qualified new hire is comfortable, productive, and committed to a long-term career.

At the same time, it's important not to treat *fit* as a code word either for blatant discrimination or subtler homogenization of work units. For example, the notion that women don't belong in stereotypically "male" jobs was discredited long ago by both court denunciations and empirical evidence. Unfortunately, that does not mean that these or similar sentiments do not continue to affect hiring decisions, and court records make clear that this includes hiring decisions in higher education. For example, hiring only people who come from similar schools or departments may act to keep out members of underrepresented groups who developed their expertise at other schools or in other settings.

Even in the absence of overt discrimination, unconscious biases can rob your department of talents and perspectives that you need to be dynamic and successful. To avoid this situation, it's critical to limit Fit Factors to those that are demonstrably essential to unit success and take steps to minimize the impact of work culture characteristics that are detrimental to success.

Evaluating your mission should naturally lead you to think about what makes your unit or institution distinct from others. A particularly important dimension is the compatibility of core values between employees and their employer (Van der Vorm, 2001). What are your organization's core values, and what do these imply about the values that potential employees need to have in order to be successful? It may not be necessary for employees to share the *identical* values, but there may be some values that are incompatible with those of your organization.

You can also ask yourself about the working climate in your department. Would you honestly characterize the working environment as formal or casual, hierarchical or participatory, high-pressure or laid-back? Are there requirements for formal attire, frequent travel, after-hours socializing, frequent overtime, or other factors that might affect which applicants would like to work in your department? Each of these work climate characteristics might suggest that employees with different characteristics and preferences may be more effective. But remember that you should emphasize only those values or personality factors that are clearly related to success at work.

Identifying Critical Performance Attributes

Once you have identified the critical tasks or outcomes associated with a job and the Risk and Fit Factors that can affect job performance, you can use this information to identify the key characteristics applicants must possess in order to be productive, satisfied, and committed. For simplicity, these characteristics, or performance attributes, are often categorized as knowledge, skills, abilities, and other characteristics, or KSAOs.

Knowledge refers to a body of information that an employee must know in order to be an effective performer. A librarian could certainly be expected to have extensive bibliographic knowledge, a research associate might be expected to understand statistical analyses, and it should go without saying that faculty are expected to be experts in their content areas.

Two caveats apply when determining knowledge requirements. The first is to limit requirements to those things a person needs to know *at the time of hire.* For some jobs, much of the necessary information is learned on the job and should not be a hiring prerequisite; making it a requirement will unnecessarily limit your pool of qualified applicants. In fact, providing on-the-job training opportunities can be an effective way of expanding an otherwise limited applicant pool. For example, schools located in rural locations may face a shortage of applicants for skilled clerical positions. Hiring and then training applicants with strong aptitudes but limited skills and experience may be a way of developing loyal (and initially less costly) employees.

The other caveat is to be cautious about using educational certificates as proxies for knowledge. Having a high school diploma, for example, tells you only that a person attended four or so years of high school; it provides no assurance that they acquired any particular knowledge that you may require. To a somewhat lesser extent, the same caution applies to college degrees.

Skill refers to proficiency performing a specific task and is a function of both underlying knowledge or ability and task-specific practice and strategies. For example, computer-programming skill requires both knowledge of one or more software languages and practice in applying that knowledge. Classroom teaching requires knowledge of the content domain, knowledge of pedagogy, an ability to understand learners' needs and translate content in a way that is understandable to each student, strategies for organizing and delivering knowledge, and substantial practice and feedback. Specifying skills as a hiring standard requires you to limit your job search to applicants who have already developed proficiency in the required skills. As with the prior example of knowledge, it's important to remember that requiring advanced skills will generally limit your applicant pool as well as increase salary expectations.

Abilities are attributes that indicate the potential to do the job, given subsequent training or experience. Although some abilities are reasonably observable (such as the ability to lift a fifty-pound load of tools and carry it up a ladder), most are more amorphous than knowledge or skills and often require a good deal of experience to estimate (Harvey, 1991). Relevant abilities may include cognitive abilities (such as the comprehension of oral or written communication, mathematical fluency, selective attention, or memory), physical abilities (such as strength or stamina), psychomotor abilities (manual dexterity, for instance) and sensory or perceptual abilities (for example, visual or auditory acuity or depth perception). Abilities are particularly important for uncertainty-based hiring, in which you are looking for potential that can be developed rather than immediate expertise. However, specifying ability rather than skill requirements also means that you will need to provide training, time, and other resources after the hire to develop the abilities into skills. For example, electricians or other skilled tradespeople may go through an apprenticeship period in which they can practice skills in a setting that is intended to provide coaching and feedback; the tenure period is intended to provide a similar setting for new faculty. On the other hand, few institutions can afford to allow a novice president to develop critical skills "on the job."

Other characteristics include any critical attributes that are not readily categorized as knowledge, skills, or abilities. Examples might include required licenses or certificates, possession of required tools, or the ability to be bonded and insured. This category also includes integrity, safety orientation, and other Risk Factor requirements, as well as values and personality characteristics that were identified as Fit Factors.

Observant readers will note that we have not included *experience* in any of the categories of attributes. The exclusion is not because experience isn't a good thing but because the label is too vague. Of what value is it to know by itself that a candidate has ten years' experience as a provost (or instructor, or department secretary, or any other position) if the candidate was an abject failure for all of those years? If *experience* really means accumulated knowledge, honed skills, established networks of contacts, or some other performance-relevant attribute, it's better to address these qualifications directly rather than using experience as a rough surrogate.

Developing a Critical Attributes List

Determining KSAO requirements for a job involves reviewing the performance foundation and asking what attributes are required of applicants, both for successful accomplishment of each critical task or outcome and for Risk and Fit Factors. An abbreviated example of a critical attributes list for a residence hall advisor position is shown in Exhibit 2.2.

In order to assure yourself (and any others with whom you may be collaborating or who may later be appraising your judgments) that you have accurately identified critical performance attributes, you should also consider

• Obtaining input from others who understand the job well. Often this is a key role of the search committee, but it may also be possible to simply talk with job incumbents or others about what they feel is essential.

- Explicitly linking each attribute back to a critical task, outcome, Risk Factor, or Fit Factor. For example, for the position of resident hall advisor you might describe problem-solving skills as a requirement dictated by such critical tasks as coordinating responses to crises. (This information could also be included in an additional column added to Exhibit 2.2.)
- Rating the importance of each attribute on a one-to-five scale with five as most critical, and focusing attention during assessment and decision making about the candidate only on attributes that are at the upper end of the scale. These ratings can also be added to your critical attributes list, as shown in Exhibit 2.2. Ratings help document that your final list of attributes represents what is truly important, and also help you limit the list of qualifications to a practical number. Although you might like to find a new assistant professor of fine arts who has an extensive portfolio of creative accomplishments, has two teaching awards, and can play three musical instruments as well as serve as department chair, it's not likely that such a candidate will be found. Focusing on what you really *need*—and then developing a secondary list of desirable but nonessential qualifications—is a better route to a successful hiring outcome.

Exhibit 2.2. Critical Attributes Analysis for Residence Hall Advisor.

Required Knowledge	*Importance*
None at time of hire	n/a
Required Skills	
Oral and written communication	4.5
Time management	4.0
Required Abilities	
Empathetic listening	5.0
Problem-solving	4.6
Other	
Honesty, integrity	4.5
Safety orientation	4.4
Clear criminal record (no relevant felony convictions)	5.0

Developing a Position Description

Once you have identified the critical tasks or outcomes you will generally want to create a job or position description. This summary can be useful for both applicants and search committee members, or for others who need an overview of the job. Since most higher education organizations probably have a template for job descriptions, we will not go into detail about what such a description should look like. In general, though, job descriptions typically include

- A formal job title

- Reporting chain (to whom the position-holders report, and who reports to them)

- A succinct (one or two sentence) statement summarizing the job responsibilities

- A listing of the critical tasks and outcomes. Optionally, a listing of noncritical tasks and outcomes that are an important but not essential part of the job

- A description of expected qualifications; these may be separated into essential and nonessential (often called "desirable") qualifications

Some authorities suggest creating two versions of the position description: a short version intended for use as an advertisement and a longer version to be used in recruiting letters sent to colleagues or to interested applicants (Waggaman, 1983).

COMPENSATION

We have left the issue of determining pay for the last section of this chapter because compensation should be to some extent a function of the demands of a job. Determining compensation is a complex topic, one that is often idiosyncratic to a particular institution's policies and practices, so our intent here is to provide some principles of how to think about compensation while conducting hiring.

Thinking About Pay and Other Rewards

One of the most difficult recruiting decisions is how to determine an appropriate level of compensation. If set too low, you will have a difficult time recruiting or retaining qualified applicants. At the same time, the costs of labor cannot exceed the value of individuals' contributions to the mission of your organization. Participating in a bidding war for a particular individual can violate this basic economic principle and create political as well as fiscal problems. For most schools, increased personnel costs can only be offset by raising tuition or by increased subsidies. Neither strategy is attractive, for going too often to either well is likely to reduce munificence down the road, whether on hiring or other activities.

The obverse problem occurs when an institution wants to conduct hiring without adequate resources. Employment offers a range of rewards, and these rewards are valued differently by different job candidates. Such differences not only make the world go 'round but also make hiring possible. Yet there are bare minima of salary, benefits, and support necessary to recruit for a given faculty position, and to try to hire in their absence wastes time and good will.

When trying to walk this fine line, it may be helpful to remember that employment is a mutual *exchange* in which employees provide contributions that meet an organization's expectations in return for inducements that meet the expectations of the jobholder. Although jobholders' expectations about compensation are ultimately based on being able to make ends meet, comparisons the candidates make among potential employers are more typically based on their evaluation of the *fairness* of pay and other outcomes.

Abundant research demonstrates that employees are very concerned about the fairness of reward *allocations* and the *process* by which these allocation decisions are made and communicated (Greenberg, 1987; Cropanzano & Greenberg, 1997). Internal equity, external equity, and employee equity are three aspects of fairness relevant to making pay decisions, each of which may have implications in different hiring situations.

- *Internal equity* refers to the fairness of pay allocations among different positions within the same organization. Internal equity is affected by decisions about the relative value of different jobs; for example, jobs requiring more education, skills, effort, or exposure to risk are more highly compensated. Internal equity is often a key factor for classified positions, for which predetermined pay grades make decisions about pay for a new position easily determined. However, internal equity is rarely a consideration for jobs in which jobholders look to an external market to establish what is fair pay (for example, faculty, administrator, and some technical positions).

• *External equity* refers to the fairness of differences in pay for the same job in different organizations. For example, faculty generally evaluate the fairness of their pay primarily with reference to colleagues in the same discipline at peer institutions, and less so with reference to faculty in other disciplines at their own institution. For positions such as these, it's important to be aware of pay levels at your peer institutions, information that is often not easy to determine. Talking with colleagues, monitoring recruiting advertisements, and participating in salary surveys that your institution or discipline may organize are ways to estimate market rates. However, since academic hiring tends to be concentrated during a short season of the year (for example, faculty hiring is most often conducted in the spring) or sporadic and idiosyncratic (as when hiring top administrators), information is often outdated or marginally relevant. For that reason, salaries listed in job announcements are often described simply as "competitive," on the assumption that by the time hiring decisions are made you will have a better sense of the compensation package you need to put together to compete in a particular labor market. Nevertheless, you need to have a pretty clear estimate up-front in order to establish a hiring budget and avoid overbidding in a hypercompetitive labor market.

• *Employee (or individual) equity* refers to the fairness of differences in pay among different individuals in the same job in the same organization. Reasons for these differences may be based on differences in qualifications (for example, a community college may be willing to pay more for an instructor with a doctoral degree than a master's degree), seniority or rank, or performance. Obviously, salaries should *not* be based on irrelevant (and illegal) characteristics such as age, gender, or race. Employee equity concerns most frequently relate to annual adjustments to salary, but these concerns can also appear in hiring scenarios as salary compression or salary inversion. Although we would normally expect individuals with more experience or higher rank to be paid more than novices, standards of external equity often conflict with employee equity; newly minted assistant professors in competitive fields sometimes receive starting salaries approaching or surpassing those of more senior and experienced faculty. Theoretically, this problem is resolved by benchmarking all jobs—not just the job being filled—to external standards and then making individual equity distinctions based on differences in performance, thereby more closely aligning differences in compensation to differences in contribution to the organization.

Considering Benefits as Part of a Total Compensation Package

Benefits such as health and life insurance, disability, and retirement also make up an important component of overall compensation. Because institutions differ in the benefits they offer, a superior benefits package can be a way to differentiate your college or university from others that a candidate may be considering. For example, your school may offer a wider choice of health plans, a larger institutional contribution to health insurance premiums, or a more generous sabbatical leave policy. These advantages may make a difference in attracting your preferred candidates, but only if you make sure they are aware of your competitive advantage in these areas. You can also create a recruiting, and retention, advantage by thinking creatively about ways to maximize tax-free or tax-sheltered income. For example, generous health benefit plans save employees out-of-pocket expenses without any increase in taxable income. Grants to support research may be another way to provide faculty with tax-free benefits. On-site day care, tuition reimbursement, or special equipment or resources may also be valued benefits for some candidates.

There may be other ways to attract particular candidates, as well as overcome limitations in budgets. Other valued outcomes of employment involve intrinsic rewards (such as the opportunity to work with outstanding colleagues and students, contribute to a particular project, or gain valuable experience), working conditions (such as flexible working schedules, sabbatical leaves, or desirable offices), and lifestyle choices (such as geographical location or the flexibility offered by not teaching in summer). Although factors such as these rarely compensate for inadequate pay or benefits, they can operate as important incentives as long as direct pay is at least at an acceptable level. Equally important, overemphasizing pay can lead to ignoring these other forms of rewards. What is critical is to get to know a candidate well enough to have an idea of what kind of creative combination of financial and nonfinancial rewards is likely to be most attractive.

SUMMARY

In this chapter you have begun the process of developing a performance-focused hiring approach. You have had the chance to develop a framework for how you want to structure the hiring process and learned how to develop a comprehensive set of critical hiring attributes based on a solid performance foundation by

- Articulating how the job contributes to the mission of your unit as well as the institution

- Describing the *essential* duties (tasks or outcomes) the jobholder must perform in order to make this contribution, as well as any Risk Factors that problem behavior on the job may create

- Determining what knowledge, skills, abilities, or other worker characteristics (KSAOs) are *essential* to perform these duties, avoid Risk Factors, or assure a good fit between candidates and the institution

- Establishing that these KSAOs are associated with the essential duties of the job and necessary at the time of hiring (rather than being learned or developed on the job)

Through this process you've gained a solid understanding of what you expect the new jobholder to contribute and what characteristics are most likely to produce excellent performance. You can use this information in the next chapter to develop a recruiting plan that will attract the high-potential applicants you're seeking.

3

Attracting Talent

FINDING AND attracting qualified applicants is one of the greatest challenges in the hiring process. Of course, there are differences in how recruiting is done for faculty, administrators, professional staff, student workers, and other kinds of jobs that exist in higher education. In this chapter we show how effective techniques for finding and attracting applicants can be applied in these different contexts. Before considering these, though, it is important to consider three basic principles for attracting talent:

- Effective hiring ultimately depends on the quality of applicants you are able to attract. You can select only from the pool of people who actually apply, and the quality of those applicants sets the upper limit for the quality of whoever is ultimately hired.

- Hiring is a mutual decision between you and potential jobholders. The entire hiring process should be conducted in a way that presents your organization as the employer of choice for qualified applicants. Remember that the hiring process itself is often a candidate's first and most vivid impression of your institution as a potential employer. Unfair, arbitrary, or offensive hiring procedures may turn away some of your best candidates.

- Desired performance, not time constraints, should guide your efforts to attract qualified workers to the fullest extent possible.

Hiring in the midst of a crisis almost inevitably compromises the quality of the person hired.

This final point is so important that we turn first to the problem of crisis hiring and how to avoid placing yourself at the mercy of a tight labor market and inflexible hiring deadlines. The rest of the chapter addresses recruiting strategies and practices that meet the first two objectives: developing a high-quality applicant pool and using the recruiting process as the initial step in creating a mutually satisfying exchange between you and those you hire.

BREAKING THE CYCLE OF CRISIS HIRING

After reading the last chapter you may be thinking, Well, this systematic and comprehensive approach to hiring sounds good, but who has the time for all that? Doing a good job of hiring *is* time-consuming, but it needs to be treated as an investment that will pay off in better employees, reduced time and resources fighting post-hiring "fires," and less time and fewer resources spent and opportunities lost in replacing people who don't pan out or who quit to find a job that suits them better.

The fire-fighting analogy is a good way to rethink the causes and cures for crisis hiring. Managers in business organizations often use the phrase "fighting fires" to describe situations where they constantly run from one hot spot to another, trying to solve problems that have suddenly erupted, with little time for planning or strategizing. In a hiring context, this may mean coming to work one morning to be surprised with a key assistant's, a trusted team member's, or a faculty member's resignation or impending departure. Your first reaction is that you need to find somebody, quickly, to fill that spot. Taking the time to think through critical attributes, develop a pool of high-potential candidates, and develop a systematic process for screening them takes a back seat to filling the position as quickly as you can.

But what if instead you "fought fires" the way professional firefighters do by anticipating that you're going to need to fight a fire in the near future, outlining what will trigger that need, planning your response, making sure you have the tools you need, and assembling them in advance so that you can respond rapidly?

Anticipation of Hiring Needs

One part of an effective hiring plan is to anticipate hiring needs, whether they are caused by growth, turnover, or activity cycles. Just as fire management professionals can anticipate—based on both history and current conditions—that wildfires are more common in August than in April and staff accordingly, there are also predictable cycles in the academic hiring arena. Hiring tenure-track faculty may be the most predictable, since most such hiring traditionally occurs in late winter or spring in anticipation of courses to be taught the following fall. A similar pattern can be seen in the hiring of many administrators. Of course, these cycles lead to a predictable problem: faculty and administrators often announce their decisions to leave too late in the hiring cycle to allow their replacement until the following year's cycle, a problem to which we will return when we discuss the concept of PATHs in the next section.

Patterns also exist in hiring for many staff positions, such as the need to increase staffing in campus bookstores when classes start or to reduce staffing in student services during breaks. For positions with multiple incumbents and regular turnover, it may be useful to track turnover incidents so that patterns over time can be detected. You can then forecast hiring needs far enough in advance to allow more systematic planning and recruitment. This process may also identify areas experiencing unusually high turnover.

Some hiring needs are based less on annual cycles than on longer-term trends in demand and supply. One example is anticipating retirements. Another example is using analysis of demographics and student interests in various fields of study to forecast enrollment, both in the aggregate and specific disciplines. Coupled with policy decisions about desirable faculty to student ratios, data about how students use campus facilities, funding, and other similar information, planners can estimate demand for faculty, staff, and student support services.

Hiring needs can also arise from anticipated growth. Planning to build a new dormitory, for example, should trigger an alarm to budget and hire for more resident advisors, cleaning and cooking staff, and so forth. Changes in curriculum—such as adding a foreign language, creative writing, or international component to students' core requirements—have an equally powerful but easily forgotten effect on demand for instructors and support staff.

Demand is only half of the equation; you also need to consider the supply of talent, both internal and external to your institution. An increase in demand may not require hiring if you are currently overstaffed (a rarity in most academic institutions) or if you can transfer qualified people from other areas (again, often difficult to do in higher education).

Projections about the internal supply of faculty and staff can be made using information about historical trends (average turnover), analysis of demographics (for example, number of employees approaching typical retirement age), and knowledge of individual jobholders' inclination to leave. Also consider the availability of external talent. (See box for an example of how demand and supply can create tremendous recruiting problems.) Hiring may be relatively easy when the external supply is plentiful and well-qualified. When qualified individuals are in scarce supply

HIRING CHALLENGES IN BUSINESS SCHOOLS

Business schools are facing a difficult hiring situation that is, in part, of their own making. Interest in business education has been on an upward trajectory for undergraduate and master's students, resulting in record demand for courses. This demand has far out-stretched what current business faculty can offer, and trying to hire additional faculty has proven to be a major challenge. In part this is because business schools cut back on Ph.D. programs in the late 1980s and 1990s as a way to cut costs; as a result the number of Ph.D.s in business increased only 3.5 percent during the 1990s, compared to fields like biology and history that saw increases of 36 and 88 percent, some of the recruiting techniques mentioned later in this chapter become particularly important.

Projections of both demand and supply often include considerable error. In the long run, though, a systematic approach will allow more effective hiring than the situation-driven, seat-of-the-pants approach that often predominates.

Unanticipated Hiring Needs and Planned Alternatives to Hiring

Despite your best efforts, unanticipated hiring needs will inevitably arise. What you want to avoid in this situation is feeling compelled to hire the first available candidate who approximately meets your hiring needs and is willing to accept the job. The key principle to remember is that you can increase the quality of your hiring by making it independent of time. Think of a graph of a normal distribution of performance. In a real-life labor market, not every point (person) on the curve is in the labor market at a given moment. So if you must hire at a particular time, you are at the mercy of the distribution in the labor market. The more you make your hiring time-independent, the more you can hire from the upper end of the distribution when candidates become available.

One way to buy yourself time to effectively hire a top candidate is to develop *Planned Alternatives to Hiring,* or PATHs. In the following sections we describe a variety of PATHs, ranging from replacement plans to temporary staffing, that may help you to defer (or even eliminate) the need to replace someone who leaves unexpectedly.

The development of a PATH begins by asking, What are the most critical consequences of a person not being available for their job? It may be helpful to break that question down into these four questions:

- What *can't* get done if this person is not in his or her job?
- Of these things, which are mission-critical?
- What is the impact on the performance of the unit?
- Over what period will the impact be felt?

The critical impact of a departure will vary by job and organizational level. In less-skilled positions, the impact typically occurs when the rate of departures reaches a level at which it becomes difficult to deliver a needed service in ways that meet quality or safety standards. With insufficient custodial staff, for example, trash piles up or entryways don't get cleared of snow and ice in the winter. Moreover, a vicious cycle can ensue, such that the remaining workers are assigned more and more work, leading them to quit as well.

In the following pages we describe five generic PATH strategies that may be appropriate in different contexts. Three of these strategies— replacement planning, succession planning, and continuous hiring— require preparation prior to the unexpected turnover. The other two strategies—job design and temporary staffing—can also serve as reactive responses to turnover.

Replacement Planning

Replacement planning answers the operational question, Who could take over tomorrow if so-and-so departed today? By having an answer to that question for the critical positions in your unit, you can reduce the uncertainty involved with unanticipated employee departures and gain more control over the timing—and quality—of hiring a replacement.

To develop your replacement plan, draw four columns on a piece of paper (or create a spreadsheet), as in the example in Exhibit 3.1. In the first column, list each position in your work group (whether that is your department, laboratory, division, or teaching unit). In the second column,

Exhibit 3.1. A Sample Replacement Plan.

Position	Primary Assignment	Primary Replacement	Secondary Replacement
Dean	Anne	Charmaine	Charles
Associate Dean of Students	Charmaine	Maureen	Charles
Associate Dean of Faculty	Charles	Maureen	Charmaine
Associate Dean of Research	Maureen	Charles	Professor Smith

write the names of the people—including yourself—who are in this work group, next to their primary job assignment. To complete the third column, ask yourself, If so-and-so was unable to be at work, who could perform that person's essential tasks? Put your answer to that question, the name of the primary replacement person, in the corresponding slot in the third column. To complete the fourth column, ask the same question again, If so-and-so was unable to be at work and his or her primary replacement wasn't available, who could perform the essential duties of the first person's job? Depending on the nature of the work, it may be useful to create two such tables, one for short-term absences and another for longer-term periods of a week to a month or academic term.

Skilled employees and those with mission-critical roles often have the kind of responsibilities for which the immediate short-term substitution provided in your replacement plans is likely to be most effective. Top administrators, ironically, are often the people for whom immediate operational replacement is less essential, because the impact of their departure is felt over a longer term. Given competent associate deans and an effective system of faculty governance, a college may be able to weather the absence of a dean better in the short term than it could the loss of a professor teaching a specialized, high-demand course or an administrative assistant who was the only one who understood how to keep a critical piece of software running.

Succession Planning

You can use your replacement plan as a starting point for a longer-term succession plan. Corporations have realized the importance of systematically developing high-potential employees into the leaders of the future. The academy, as a whole, has been less successful in this endeavor, particularly when it comes to identifying and developing leadership potential among faculty. As a result, academic departments often have weak management infrastructures, which make it particularly difficult to cope with turnover of department chairs, associate deans, and other "quasi-management" positions. Succession plans can help you identify talent gaps and develop strategies for filling them with existing employees where possible, thus reducing the need to hire externally when a key employee leaves.

Taking a strategic approach to succession planning offers particular benefits for faculty staffing, since the quality (and mix) of faculty can often make or break a department's reputation. Retirement times are known years in advance in institutions outside the United States, and even in the United States are generally predictable within a few years. In either situation, there is a clear long-range pattern of who will retire from a department in what order. Armed with this information, succession planning provides the opportunity to think through and begin to implement new directions for a department. If there will be three people retiring in botany, for example, each position need not necessarily be filled in the same specialty as the current incumbent. By planning ahead the department might, for example, decide to replace one systematist with another, make sure that a second position is filled to cover a gap in molecular biology, and keep the third position flexible over the time of the three retirements to look for an outstanding senior person.

To create a succession plan, begin with a given position in your work group and ask who might be possible successors. You can create a development and succession plan that helps the intended successor or successors begin to receive training or experience necessary for the position, and sometimes fill the position on a temporary or acting basis. In a sense, a succession plan is similar to the coaching that takes place in an effective promotion and tenure system, except that it more specifically targets organizational needs (such as building management skills) rather than the individual contributor skills (such as research and teaching) that most promotion and tenure systems emphasize.

An advantage of succession planning is that it tends to encourage internal promotion. At the same time, succession planning will help you see where your unit lacks depth—where you need to be prepared to go outside for a successor. Your succession plan also helps make your decision to promote internally or recruit externally understandable and fair to others in your work group. If a possible successor lacks specific training or experience, then you and the potential successor can agree to focus in that direction. If there are no internal successors, then you will want to create a strategy (described in a later section) that includes having an interim internal replacement who can perform critical tasks at a minimal level, while also attracting a fully qualified replacement.

Continuous Hiring

Continuous hiring is a strategy of hiring outstanding candidates when they become available, whether or not there is an immediate need for them. Continuous hiring and succession planning are variations on the same principle: make your hiring as time-independent as possible so that you can hire outstanding candidates when they become available. Continuous hiring is most appropriate when the same position is held by a large number of employees and you anticipate ongoing turnover. Therefore, it is generally not as appropriate as succession planning for hiring administrators or faculty, though it can be a very useful strategy for some staff positions. Continuous hiring of top-notch candidates can be particularly effective when there is a significant difference between the minimal and desirable qualifications for the job.

The challenge with continuous hiring, of course, is what to do with a new employee that you don't immediately need. One possibility is for the employee to start with part-time or short-term work, which can serve in part as a job trial. A second option—more likely to be mutually acceptable—is for the employee to come to work for necessary training, which should then be combined with a job trial. In positions with larger numbers of employees and higher rates of turnover, you may be able to predict whether a position is likely to open up during the training and job trial period. A third possibility is to use the new hire in a "utility" position until a specific position becomes available. To make the hire more attractive, you could offer the new hire the options of taking the first position that comes open, or use the utility position to let the employee identify the job or unit in which the employee is most interested. The fourth option is to use continuous hiring to actively manage the quality of performance in your work group, rather than waiting for an opening to occur. Specifically, once you have hired and trained an outstanding candidate and are comfortable with the results of any job trial, ask yourself if there are workers with substandard performance who need to reduce their hours, upgrade their performance, transfer to a better job match, or find employment elsewhere.

Replacement and succession planning, PATHS, and continuous hiring all require various levels of preplanning. The remaining two options—job redesign and use of temporary staffing—can also be done on a proactive basis but are often used after an employee has unexpectedly departed.

Job Design

Suppose a person quits, you have no replacement available, and there is no viable PATH in place. One possibility is to redesign how the work performed by the person gets done. In fact, the loss of an employee is always an opportunity to rethink work design and flow. Sometimes technology can be used to perform some of the tasks the person did manually, and can either eliminate the need for that portion of the job or make it easier for someone else to take it on. In other cases, the person's tasks can be redistributed among others. On a temporary basis, these kinds of job changes can buy time to effectively recruit a replacement; in a few cases you may even discover that some of the tasks are no longer relevant and that the job, or parts of it, can be eliminated.

You can also use proactive job design to avoid having a crisis when a person leaves. Designing jobs to assure cross-functional capabilities increases your PATH options for any of the jobs in the set. For example, in an admissions office there may be individuals whose responsibilities include marketing the program, providing information to potential applicants, processing admission applications, and preprocessing financial aid. This role specialization may be optimal for daily operations, but ensuring that individuals rotate across at least a subset of the positions provides more variety for the employees and more flexibility to your PATH if a person is unavailable to work for any reason.

Temporary Staffing

When your options for in-house alternatives are limited, your PATH may consist of staffing a position with a temporary worker while a permanent replacement is found. Temporary workers, when dealt with effectively, may be just as committed as regular employees (Miller, 1995). This can apply to adjunct and visiting faculty, as well as to temporary office workers and finance and accounting specialists. It can also apply to senior members of the university who fill administrative roles on a temporary basis, typically senior faculty or retired administrators who may be willing to "step in" for a short term but who have no long-term interest in the position. In other cases, "temporary-to-permanent" arrangements—hiring as regular employees the temporary employees who are good performers and are interested in regular employment—may provide an effective way to conduct both continuous hiring and job trials.

A particularly common variant of temporary staffing involves the deployment of nonregular faculty for teaching positions (Leatherman, 2000; Wilson, 1999). These faculty may include graduate teaching assistants, adjunct faculty, and instructors on short-term contracts. In addition to the added staffing flexibility they allow, such arrangements can provide training for graduate students, a diversity of perspectives from nontraditional instructors, and a corps of individuals especially dedicated to the teaching mission of your school.

However, the prolonged use of nonregular employees—at any level—should always be part of a well thought out staffing plan and not simply a way to manipulate personnel budgets. Failing to use temporary staffing strategically can leave these individuals feeling exploited while also creating gaps in other performance domains, such as development of research and administrative leadership.

Anticipating hiring needs and preplanning strategies for responding to unanticipated hiring needs are the first steps in making hiring more time-independent and focused on quality. The next step is to take advantage of this increased time-independence to develop a strategy for effectively attracting high-potential applicants.

BUILDING YOUR RECRUITING FOUNDATION

The basic question to ask as you plan your recruiting efforts is, Why would qualified applicants want to work here rather than at another institution or employer? To answer this question, you need to ask two others: What do qualified workers want? What do we have to offer?

The first step is to list the factors that make the job, your institution, or the work in general desirable to the kinds of applicants you want to hire. Second, list the factors that make the job, institution, or work undesirable. Third, make a smaller list of factors that are most important to potential employees in deciding about a job. These critical factors should be the focus in your recruiting efforts. They can also help you analyze your organizational practices for changes that would make the job more attractive to qualified candidates.

The Importance of Becoming an Employer of Choice

An employer of choice is an employer within a set of institutions, a discipline, or a geographic area that first comes to mind when a candidate is asked, Where would you really like to work? Employers of choice have a huge advantage when it comes to attracting top talent; the information collected in your recruiting self-analysis can help your unit or institution become such an employer.

Your task is clearly much easier if your self-analysis reveals an abundance of features that top candidates want and an absence of negatives. Such a situation only occurs with substantial effort, so let's consider two options for dealing with a shortage of positives or an excess of negatives. The obvious option is to either remove negative features or to add desirable ones, particularly positive features that are clearly related to performance. Making such changes is one of the most effective strategies to increase the long-term quality of candidates and your workforce. When this isn't possible, though, or is impractical in the time frame of recruiting for a current hire, the second option is to objectively describe both the desirable and undesirable factors about a job and work environment in a *realistic job preview.*

Realistic Job Previews

Realistic job previews are an approach to recruiting that recognizes that hiring is a two-way process that involves decisions by both the candidates and the hiring organization. It's tempting to emphasize only the most positive aspects of a job to make it more attractive to potential applicants. But doing so is likely to cause dissatisfaction—maybe even a sense of betrayal or fraud—once the person takes the job and experiences the truth. Morale problems and heightened turnover result. Anytime you're experiencing turnover in the first six months or so of a job (or the first year or two in the case of faculty and administrators) you should ask yourself whether your recruiting can benefit from a realistic job preview.

A realistic job preview gives candidates an accurate and representative overview of both the strengths and limitations of a job, and typically results in more satisfied employees who have greater trust in administration and are less likely to quit (Wanous, 1980). Realistic job previews tend to be most effective in competitive labor markets in which applicants actually have choices and can use the information to make an informed decision. People may then "self-select" themselves out of jobs in which they would be less satisfied. This reduces costly turnover, but it also requires expanding recruiting efforts to offset a higher rate of applicants not accepting job offers.

To prepare a realistic job preview, return to the aspects of the job that your recruiting self-analysis showed were important to potential workers—positive or negative. By all means stress the positive aspects—particularly those that are salient to a specific candidate—when describing the job. Where your analysis showed less desirable aspects of a job, especially when these are truly inherent in the nature of the work, you should describe those aspects, too, making sure to do so in neutral language.

Providing a balanced perspective can seem self-defeating, especially when it's been difficult to find qualified applicants or when you really want a particular candidate to accept your offer. When you find yourself tempted to gild the lily, remind yourself how much work you've invested in the search and ask yourself if you really want to go through that again in a year after your candidate develops reality shock and departs. Helping applicants match themselves with a job or work climate in which they'll be satisfied and productive pays dividends for both parties.

DEVELOPING A RECRUITING REPERTOIRE

How do you find good applicants once you've managed to avoid crisis hiring and have completed your recruiting self-analysis? Whether you're hiring an administrative assistant, an assistant professor, or a university president, keep this recruiting tip in mind: *The best person for the job may not be looking for a job, much less this job.* Placing an ad in the *Chronicle of Higher Education,* your professional group's placement roster, or the regional newspaper may not suffice when it comes to attracting this individual. In addition to such approaches, you need to ask, How can I locate people who might make good candidates—even if they're not currently looking for work?

For many academic jobs, the answer is to use the networking opportunities that are part of our workaday lives: conferences, committees within professional associations, and conversations with colleagues about who might be interested in and qualified for your job opening. You can bolster these approaches by building recruiting networks before you actually need them through activities such as

- Hosting professional meetings or events at your institution

- Attending or supporting civic organizations that appeal to a range of participants or targeted groups

- Hosting an open house in your institution or work group, either for workers in the needed specialty or for the broad community

- Sponsoring organizations that serve underrepresented groups; for example, female engineers, faculty of color, or individuals with disabilities

- Scheduling interviews or lunches with targeted individuals

- Pushing for new avenues and approaches to reach qualified applicants of whom you're unaware

Developing a long-term approach to attracting candidates—without regard to whether they are looking for work—should form the foundation of your recruiting repertoire. If you are using continuous hiring, the contacts you make will provide you with some candidates for hiring. If not, you have a group of candidates and contacts to turn to when a hiring event occurs.

The biggest shortcoming about recruiting by "traditional" networking is that you potentially limit your contacts to people you know or are more likely to meet. Because there's no particular reason to assume that all qualified applicants for a position are likely to know you, such networking can actually narrow your pool along a non-performance-related criterion. So as important as networking is, you need to complement it with other recruiting strategies, such as classified ads, employee referrals, and search firms.

Classified Advertising

Classified advertising allows you to broaden your applicant pool to include individuals outside your own circle of contacts. You can use it to target certain types of applicants by advertising in particular trade publications or professional journals. This can help increase the diversity of your applicant pool, for instance by advertising in sources read by female or minority applicants. Advertising can also be a good way to document both the specific requirements of the job and your efforts to reach an appropriate pool of applicants; for this reason, posting a job in some written media is generally standard practice.

There are also disadvantages to classified advertising. Costs can be high, so the *cost-effectiveness* of different advertising media is crucial in terms of bringing you qualified applicants. Campus papers may be cost-effective means for recruiting locally, for example, but make little sense for national searches.

The sheer volume of responses generated can be another disadvantage of classified ads. In general, increasing the number of responses of qualified applicants allows you to be more selective. Along with this opportunity comes the logistical burden of responding to all the applicants. Although easy to put off, it is essential to respond to applicants regardless of whether you are seriously interested in them. Doing so is courteous, helps maintain a good relationship with applicants who may be potential future candidates, and maintains good relationships with your community, be it a local geographical community or a larger professional community.

When writing your advertisement, communicate what you are looking for in performance-oriented language, focusing on key duties that produce critical outcomes, key attributes needed to perform the key duties effectively, and key factors that realistically describe the job. Write the ad emphasizing the critical information that will help potential applicants to realistically

- Differentiate the job you are advertising from other jobs they might also be considering

- Evaluate the factors that will be essential for success at the job against their own qualifications

- Make a realistic decision about whether to apply

Think about the advertisement from the applicant's point of view, not yours. As one example, it is generally useful to provide the salary range for a position, particularly if the position is one that may attract applicants with widely varying expectations about pay. With this information, individuals with salary expectations that are incompatible with your resources will not apply, thus saving you both the time and potential embarrassment of pursuing a candidate who you would be unable to hire. Expectations can be a particular issue when applicants lack higher education experience and may overestimate pay levels in colleges and universities.

Internet Recruiting

The line between traditional classified ads and Internet postings continues to blur. Even if you are not posting jobs electronically, a second party may be doing so for you, and job applicants are surely exploring your Web pages for more information. You will certainly want to post professional openings with appropriate professional associations, where placement activities continue to move from paper to the Web to increase efficiency and lower costs. Intranets provide a convenient means of posting positions internally.

Because most institutions of higher education have already invested in information technology, the Internet provides a potent complement to traditional advertising. It allows you to provide more background information about your school than would be feasible in traditional ads. Since most savvy applicants will be accessing this information anyway, you want to provide a central site for the position that facilitates applicants' search for other relevant information about the department, the institution, and the local community. When creating such a site, consider these points:

- Use guidelines similar to classified advertising: emphasize the information that will most help applicants differentiate you from other employers, focusing in particular on characteristics that are most likely to appeal to the best applicants.

- Internet recruiting is frequently considered impersonal, particularly for organizations that require that application materials be submitted electronically. One solution is to offer a specific contact, preferably with both phone and e-mail information, for interested individuals to contact. If you do offer an e-mail route, you need to be prepared to reply to applications and queries promptly.

- Material received, and material you transmit in response, should be considered to be public information, not necessarily subject to the same privacy protections as documents transmitted through the mail.

- Work closely with the system administrators in your organization to make sure that any interactive parts of your recruiting effort (such as electronic résumé submission) are developed with the security of your own organization's computing resources in mind. They may also be helpful for ensuring that Web materials have a professional look and feel, characteristics that can have a significant impact on applicants' overall perceptions of your school.

Employee Referrals

Employee referrals are a straightforward extension of the networking concept, in which employees are encouraged to refer people they feel would be good candidates for employment (Morgan & Smith, 1996). Because current employees are likely to understand the technical and cultural aspects of a job, and have an interest in having fellow employees who pull their own weight and add to the credibility of your unit, they may be more likely to refer friends and associates who will be more productive and less likely to quit.

Employee referrals can also be an inexpensive recruiting method, though this depends on whether or not you provide a bonus for referrals. Among for-profit companies (and some nonprofits, such as hospitals), it has become increasingly common for employees to receive a financial incentive for applicants they refer who are hired and stay with the company. This idea has not yet caught on in academia, but may be worth considering for positions that are in high demand. Information technology (IT) positions, for example, are still difficult to fill even as the labor market fluctuates. Employee referrals can help persuade IT workers to seek a position at an academic institution instead of at a software company. However, you want to make sure that the bonus does not distort employees' motivation for participating; you want employees to refer candidates because the candidate is qualified, not simply to obtain a bonus. If you do offer a bonus, make sure that it's paid soon enough to be meaningful to the referring employee.

The success of employee referral programs depends on effective implementation. Employee referrals tend to work best when you

- Encourage high-performing employees to make referrals. It does you little good to have a group of poor performers refer people they would like to work with.

- Provide referring employees with information about the critical performance attributes for the job. Make sure they know that you will be hiring on the basis of those attributes.

- Encourage referring employees to think broadly and refer people they think have these key attributes—not just people they know and like.

- Supplement employee referrals with other forms of recruiting that will reach a broader, more diverse pool of applicants.

Search Firms

Effective recruiting is a lot of work, particularly when the pool of available and qualified candidates is small, hidden, or nonexistent. Faced with this daunting challenge, colleges and universities increasingly turn to external search firms specializing in academic searches, particularly for positions such as presidents, chancellors, and provosts. Similar employment agencies are used for professional positions that occur in both higher education and other fields, such as information technology professionals, accounting staff, and medical professionals.

Search firms are vendors who provide candidates to you in exchange for a fee. Frequently mentioned advantages of search firms and employment agencies are the applicant pools they already have in place (or can obtain quickly), the prescreening they can provide, and the ability of the firm to replace your time and effort with theirs. The most commonly cited disadvantage is the cost.

Central to evaluating the advantages and disadvantages of search firms and employment agencies is understanding that a *vendor relationship* exists between your institution and the firm, and that there may be a conflict between your institution's best interests and those of the vendor. It is almost always in a search firm's best interest that you hire a given candidate they provide, but doing so is not always in your interests. In fact, short-sighted search firms may be tempted to recommend a candidate who is likely to move on to another position in a short time, since doing so may provide them with an opportunity for repeat business, possibly with the same institution, who now needs to find a new administrator, as well as by recommending the departing administrator to a new client school.

When deciding whether to use a search firm or employment agency, recognize that you will need to put time and work into evaluating the search firm *in addition* to the time you still need to invest in identifying the desired characteristics for the position and in making a final decision about who to hire. If you will put more work into selecting an agency than you will into recruiting and selecting an employee, and if the final pool of applicants would be much the same, why not do the search yourself?

If you decide to use an outside vendor, use the same care in choosing the vendor that you would in choosing an employee. Ask for specifics on how applicants are recruited and screened. As you would with any other vendor, look for a quality process, a quality product, fair and understandable pricing, and ethical business practices.

If you are using a search firm or employment agency, it is also critical that you, and any search committee or governing board, not abdicate ultimate responsibility to the firm for the hiring decision. Use such firms to help obtain applicants but not to make critical decisions about the future of your institution.

ENHANCING DIVERSITY IN HIGHER EDUCATION THROUGH RECRUITING, RETENTION, AND TALENT FLOW

Developing a diverse workforce has become a critical priority for U.S. employers, and the challenge to do so is significant in higher education. Developing a diverse workforce is more than a hiring issue; to do so effectively requires an integrative approach that spans hiring, performance management, and retention of high-performing workers. We refer to this integrative approach as *talent flow*: the notion that effective management of talent requires an analysis of the individual, environmental, and organizational factors that influence the flow of individuals into, through, and out of your organization (Levin & Rosse, 2001).

In general, higher education is characterized by *slow talent flow*. This means that people who are hired at higher education institutions may or may not work out initially, but if they are successful they often stay at that institution for many years. This effect is amplified by institutional or civil service personnel systems, as well as by the tenure system for faculty.

Although slow talent flows have some advantages, they also present one of the primary challenges for developing a diverse and effective workforce. In part this is because the composition today of your school's staff and faculty very likely reflects the demographics and social characteristics of several years ago. Because turnover is relatively low for many positions, there are few opportunities to increase diversity, even with affirmative action or diversity programs.

A second and related challenge to increasing diversity is that in many faculty and administrative positions the absolute number of candidates from nontraditional or underrepresented backgrounds actively in the labor market at any given time may be low. These low absolute numbers combine with the slow talent flow to create a potentially difficult hiring situation: your institution may not be hiring when talented candidates are in the labor market and looking around, and there may seem to be few such candidates in the labor market when you are hiring. This situation provides yet another example of the importance of making your hiring as independent as possible of time pressures, since there is perhaps no more efficacious strategy for increasing the diversity of your workforce.

The principles of talent flow combine with the conditions of slow talent flow in higher education to produce one particularly effective strategy for developing a diverse workforce: the effort you put into helping new hires succeed—and then retaining them—will have a far greater long-term impact on the diversity of your workforce than the raw number of candidates who are initially hired from diverse backgrounds. Why? Because the long-term levels of talent in your workforce (including talent from underrepresented groups) result more from the length of time people stay than from the number of people you initially hire (Levin & Rosse, 2001).

Consider two simple examples. In the first example, University A implements a crash diversity hiring program and hires twenty candidates per year from underrepresented groups. However, since their focus is on diversity rather than long-term performance, not all the candidates are hired on the basis of a solid match with job requirements. Moreover, University A has a "sink or swim" mentality when it comes to performance management, and a culture that is not supportive of nontraditional employees or students. The result after seven years is that only a few of the 140 or so targeted hires are still with the university, and everyone—including potential jobholders—has developed a bad impression of the university's diversity program.

University B, on the other hand, takes a more methodical approach to increasing the diversity of their faculty. They work hard at recruiting candidates who are a good match with their culture and job requirements, and they foster a supportive approach to mentoring all new faculty and increasing the proportion of faculty who are successfully tenured and who stay at the university after receiving tenure. As less of the diversity budget goes into targeted hiring and more into retention efforts that are consistent with the university's commitment to all new faculty, University B hires only ten faculty from nontraditional backgrounds per year. Yet the majority of these hires are successful performers as a result of University B's commitment to developing successful new faculty, and many of these choose to stay in the supportive environment in which they have thrived. As a result, much larger proportions and absolute numbers of faculty hired by University B from nontraditional and underrepresented backgrounds will be employed at the end of the same seven-year period. Moreover, University B will gain a reputation as a university with a fundamental commitment to success and to diversity.

Earlier in the chapter we discussed the importance of expanding your applicant pool; this approach is particularly important for adding diversity to faculty and administration hires. In faculty hiring, this means putting in the personal footwork to develop effective relationships with young scholars from diverse backgrounds when they're still undergraduates, graduate students, initially on the job market, working at postdocs, or similar placements. Taking the time to develop effective relationships early on and contribute to the career development of an individual will increase the likelihood that such an individual will want to work at your institution.

Personal connections, of course, are by no means the sole test by which any candidate selects your institution. Candidates will want to be certain, for example, that the basic package of compensation and benefits offered meets their needs. Beyond compensation, it's worthwhile to use the methods described elsewhere in the chapter to frankly assess the characteristics of your institution that may be particularly salient for attracting or repelling a candidate you want to recruit. As we've noted, one of the most salient factors is the probability of success on the job. If you can demonstrate that your institution has gone to some length to make it likely for qualified new jobholders to succeed, that commitment can go a long way in attracting a candidate.

SUMMARY

Attracting qualified applicants is critical to performance-based hiring, because the quality of applicants sets the upper limit for the effectiveness of your hiring. If you've recruited only mediocre applicants, no amount of interviewing, testing, or background checking will allow you to hire excellent candidates.

Developing an adequate applicant pool can be particularly difficult when hiring is a result of the unexpected departure of jobholders. It's important to develop contingency plans for dealing with turnover. Developing some planned alternatives to hiring (PATHs) allows you make the best hiring decisions even under difficult conditions. Preparing a replacement plan helps remove the operational crises experienced when an employee quits, allowing more time to plan the hiring of a replacement. Succession planning, continuous hiring, job redesign, and temporary staffing are other options that can be used to improve the quality of your workforce.

A second step is to develop a sound recruiting strategy, preferably before a hiring need occurs. This step involves analyzing your job and organization from the perspective of applicants. Determine what factors are likely to appeal to them and what factors are likely to be concerns among the most qualified applicants, and make whatever changes you can in order to become an employer of choice. Then present applicants with a balanced picture that will allow them to make an informed decision about whether there is a good match between themselves, the job, and your institution.

The third step is to use effective recruiting practices matched to the requirements of your institution and the job for which you are hiring. Your goal is to develop the broadest possible range of qualified applicants from which to choose. Making sure your recruiting is fair and reaches out to qualified applicants increases the quality of the candidates and helps you ensure that your recruiting efforts—along with your entire hiring system—operate legally, the subject of the next chapter.

4

The Legal and Social Context of Hiring

IDENTIFYING, ATTRACTING, and hiring the right talent has always been a challenge, but today the process can seem even more daunting because of legal and ethical concerns. Academic administrators sometimes dread hiring because it has become not only the target of legal challenges but also a source of internal disputes, sanctions, and conflicts. Rather than asking, What characteristics are most critical for making a good hire? it is easy to instead fixate on legal constraints on what you can or cannot say, ask, or do while interacting with job applicants.

Hiring in an academic environment can be particularly challenging from a legal perspective. In a small private-sector company, hiring decisions are often made informally. This can increase the exposure to legal risks, yet small organizations may be exempt from many legal requirements. In large private-sector companies and in traditional civil service hiring, the hiring process is rigidly controlled, and positions and relevant qualifications are also carefully defined. Academic hiring often involves an intriguing combination of the two approaches. On the one hand, the hiring process is often prescribed, for instance, in the structure of search committees or the way that positions must be advertised. On the other hand, the nature of academic work is that many jobs are left inadequately defined, and the decision process itself in academic hiring is often quite arbitrary.

The theme of this chapter is that the legal and social context of employment, both before and after hiring, is a reality that colleges and universities cannot and should not avoid, but that it need not interfere with the hiring of effective employees. Instead, we see performance-based hiring as complementary to relevant legal, moral, and ethical standards. When specific questions or challenges appear, it is always a good idea to work closely with legal counsel well versed in employment law. Such individuals, sometimes assigned as *ex officio* members of search committees, can also be very helpful for providing updates and summaries of local as well as federal equal employment laws. But on a day-to-day basis a good rule of thumb is to ask yourself two questions: (1) whether your decisions and actions are truly focused on performance rather than on non-performance-based factors, and (2) can the decisions you make and the actions you take be justified to six strangers sitting in a jury box. Acting fairly and consistently and making decisions on the basis of job performance are essential for making that case.

The purpose of this chapter is to provide a layperson's description of the legal and social context of hiring to guide you through the rest of the book's descriptions of hiring practices. In the next section we provide an overview of the various sources of employment law, with a primary emphasis on federal equal employment opportunity (EEO) regulations. We next explore the process by which a discrimination claim is made. You will gain a better understanding of how to conduct the hiring process both effectively and legally by comprehending how an aggrieved applicant gathers evidence of discrimination and what your institution would need to do to defend against such a charge.

THE SOCIAL CONTEXT OF HIRING LAWS

Early examples of employment legislation, concerning such issues as wages, hours, and health and safety, focused on improving working conditions for all workers. During the 1950s and 1960s, the civil rights movement highlighted the disparities in how the benefits of employment were spread across society. Resulting equal employment opportunity legislation was designed to open access to desirable employment to a much larger proportion of the workforce.

One of the pernicious effects of discrimination is to artificially restrict labor pools, generally to white male applicants without disabilities. EEO laws provide for a larger pool of qualified applicants who might otherwise have been overlooked for reasons that had nothing to do with their performance potential. These laws also remind us of the need to select applicants on the basis of legitimate, job-related factors—the same factors that underlie the performance-based hiring that forms the foundation of this book.

Let's consider some examples of the kinds of hiring issues that arise today in academic institutions, and how they can be addressed from legal, ethical, and performance perspectives.

We're down to two finalists for the assistant professor position in sociology. One of them has more publications and better teaching experience, but the other person has a Ph.D. from a university with a better reputation. We're going for the second person, because it's hard to argue with a good pedigree.

I can't believe my luck! After the last director of corporation and foundation relations left on short notice, I received an application from a candidate who's got everything I'm looking for. Willie has an MBA from a top school, ten years' experience in a similar position at a nationally renowned university, and dynamite connections with some of the best companies in the state. There's just one problem; when I checked about that last job, there was a hint that he had been sexually harassing his female assistant. But the provost loves the guy and is putting pressure on me to increase my fundraising . . . and now.

We realized that we have too few deans who are women, so we made a special effort to recruit Barbara when we were hiring a new dean for the law school. But now James, the internal candidate, is threatening to charge us with reverse discrimination. We're damned if we do and damned if we don't.

Kwan has been employed as a part-time instructor for two years, and seems to be doing a great job. He knows his stuff, and when other faculty have visited his class they've come away impressed with his teaching skills. But English is not his first language, and a number of students— and their parents—have complained that he's hard to understand. His accent *is* a bit heavy, but the complaints seem to come predominantly from students who aren't so comfortable with people who are "different" from the mostly white, middle-class community our college is in. I think Kwan would be a great hire, but I can't afford to alienate parents and future alumni, especially now that we're in the middle of a program review.

When faced with situations like these, there are at least three perspectives to help you decide on a suitable course of action: (1) determining what response is most appropriate from a *performance orientation*; (2) identifying what relevant *legal requirements* dictate; and (3) deciding what approach is most compatible with relevant *ethical standards*. Much of the time these perspectives will lead to nearly the same decision, but differences exist often enough to make it worthwhile to understand each perspective.

The Performance Perspective

As we described in Chapter Two, hiring decisions should be based on contribution to the performance of the organization. The fundamental question is whether the capabilities you are basing your hiring decisions on are really essential to job performance. Consider, for example, the department chair who's leaning toward the sociology professor with the degree from the well-known institution over the candidate with the better record. Like many situations in which the performance criterion is subtly diluted, this one has a very attractive facade. Hiring graduates of "top programs" brings both prestige and comfort, but it does not necessarily bring top talent.

Part of what makes this facade comfortable is the assumption that top schools select only the best candidates and then provide them with the very best training, an assumption that is probably true in general but may be incorrect in particular cases. Even in the best of circumstances mistakes in selection occur, and we all know that "mistakes" in graduate education also occur. Thus, while the overall probability of obtaining a successful hire may be higher with graduates of a top program, there is no guarantee of that. Quality of program may be one factor to consider, but a stronger predictor of future performance is likely to be more direct measures of critical performance attributes.

The other aspect of what makes hiring the candidate with a better "pedigree" more comfortable may be that he or she is more similar to you or to others in the department. We're naturally attracted to people who are like ourselves, and this may be a particular temptation for faculty, who often grow accustomed to "cloning" themselves when training grad students. But fundamentally, it is no different from giving preference to sorority sisters or your neighbor's child when the preference is based on similarity rather than job-relevant attributes. Moreover, preference for those who are similar may raise legal, as well as performance, issues when it leads to gender, race, or other forms of discrimination. Targeting critical performance attributes—whether regular attendance, an excellent research record, or administrative skills—keeps you focused on the qualifications that are job-related and readily defended should a legal challenge arise.

Our own approach is to rely primarily on the performance perspective. Its emphasis on job-relatedness also forms the core of the legal and ethical perspectives we describe next, and it capitalizes on what you know as an academic manager, rather than forcing you to rely too much on legal advice in trying to formulate hiring decisions. Nevertheless, there are times when the other perspectives are important complements to the performance perspective.

The Moral-Ethical Perspective

A performance orientation shouldn't be confused with an expedient, "bottom line" approach to difficult ethical questions. Take the case of Willie, the candidate for corporate relations director who may have been harassing one of his staff. A cynical view of performance orientation might lead to the conclusion that Willie is otherwise so qualified that it would be acceptable to overlook his transgressions, or to hope that he's learned from his past. But if doing so meant that he would be put in a position of power from which more women could be his targets, it would be a hard decision to support. It could also have longer-term performance implications, particularly if he continued his behavior and the word got out that you had hired him despite his past behavior.

The Legal Perspective

The legal perspective is often important when determining the best *means* of reaching performance objectives. In other words, once you know *what* you are looking for in applicants, legal considerations may affect *how* you assess these factors. For example, you'll learn in Chapter Five that interview questions about attendance should be worded so as to avoid the inference that women are more likely than men to miss work due to child care responsibilities.

One drawback of the legal perspective is that it can too easily distract you from performance issues. For example, federal antidiscrimination law includes an exemption that allows religiously affiliated organizations to base hiring decisions in part on the religion of applicants, whereas discrimination on the basis of religion is prohibited for most organizations. The logic is that in some cases there may be a legitimate case that only individuals sharing the religious values and beliefs of a religiously affiliated institution can be an effective employee. Although that may be true in some situations, schools may be tempted to use that exemption to justify discrimination that could not be justified on a performance basis. For many jobs in a religiously affiliated university, one's creed has little tangible relation to job performance. Using the law to discriminate may reduce effectiveness if more effective applicants are passed over because they have the "wrong" set of beliefs.

Another way that the legal perspective can be distracting is when it leads to an overemphasis on legal risks. Deciding not to check references because doing so might create legal challenges—even if references are a valid source of essential information about an applicant—is abdicating your fundamental responsibility to hire qualified people. Risks of lawsuits (or other adverse consequences) are part of many administrative decisions, but they need to be weighed against the potential benefits. The risk involved in the day-to-day operation of any college or university is far greater than the legal risks during hiring, so long as you follow basic practices for reducing and managing risks of hiring. Conversely, if you conduct your hiring in a way that doesn't focus on performance, isn't systematic, and isn't explicit about making effective decisions, you won't be likely to make effective hires, and you will have greater exposure to legal action.

WHERE DO ALL THESE RULES COME FROM?

Legal guidelines affecting hiring emanate from a variety of sources. Beginning with a broad overview of these guidelines may help explain how cases develop and why the responsibilities of different types of academic organizations may sometimes vary. Although we will focus primarily on state and federal laws, we note that most colleges and universities have created their own regulations, which you will want to become familiar with, to ensure compliance with legal and social mandates.

One major category of legal guidelines involves *constitutional law,* either at the federal or state level. Because constitutional provisions apply to public sector organizations, they are of particular concern to state colleges and universities. Like other state institutions, these schools are governed by the Fourteenth Amendment's guarantee of equal protection under the law, as well as by constitutional protections against unlawful search and seizure (a potential issue in drug testing, for example). Additional protections may be based in the constitution of the state in which your school is located (for example, California's constitution provides a broader set of privacy protections than does the U.S. Constitution).

The second category includes *statutory law,* that is, laws that are written by elected representatives to federal or state congressional bodies. Exhibit 4.1 lists the key federal EEO laws and briefly summarizes their requirements. Although these laws provide the underpinning for the rest of the chapter, it's worth remembering that protections provided in state and local laws may be more encompassing than those provided in federal law.

Common law refers to laws handed down through judicial decisions. Precedents created by different jurisdictions and levels of the judicial

Exhibit 4.1. Major Federal Equal Employment Laws.

Federal Statute	Provisions
Age Discrimination in Employment Act (amended 1987)	Prohibits discrimination on the basis of age for employees aged forty or over.
Americans with Disabilities Act (Title I) (1990)	Prohibits discrimination on the basis of disabilities that are not related to essential duties of the job. Requires reasonable accommodation of otherwise qualified employees.
Civil Rights Act (Title VII) (amended 1991)	Prohibits discrimination in all aspects of employment on the basis of race, color, religion, national origin, or gender.
Equal Pay Act (1963)	Prohibits gender-based discrimination in pay.
Immigration Reform and Control Act (1986)	Requires employers to verify employment eligibility for all job applicants. Prohibits discrimination on basis of national origin.
Pregnancy Discrimination Act (1978)	Prohibits discrimination on the basis of pregnancy or pregnancy-related conditions. Covered employees must be treated in accordance with an organization's short-term disability provisions.

system create a complex patchwork of requirements that evolve over time and may differ across states or judicial districts. Keeping updated on these changes is another reason that it is useful to consult with legal counsel. Three aspects of common law are particularly relevant to hiring and other personnel decisions:

- *Tort law* concerns situations in which a person can be held liable for intentional harm inflicted on another. An example is the possibility that a previous employer may be held responsible for defamation of an applicant's character when providing false, unfavorable information during a reference check.

- *Contract law* determines the conditions under which an agreement (such as an agreement to be hired) is legally binding. Contract law is an important consideration when describing terms and conditions of employment to a new hire; be sure that you are not unintentionally implying contractual obligations that you do not intend to honor.

- *The common law of agency* describes situations in which an employer is responsible for actions taken by its agents, such as department chairs who may be asking illegal questions in employment interviews. In general, employers may be liable for the actions or promises of employees acting in a supervisory capacity.

With this quick overview in mind, we can review the key provisions of the major laws. Once again, our purpose is to provide a working understanding of the key provisions of the laws, not to dwell on the intricacies that may affect particular situations.

WHAT IS PROHIBITED?

Generally speaking, the intent of EEO laws is to prohibit discrimination based on certain "protected characteristics." These characteristics include

- Race or color
- Gender (including pregnancy)

- Religion

- National origin

- Age (anyone over forty years of age)

- Disabilities

The previous paragraph includes two important but subtle points. One is that we prefer the term "protected characteristics" to the more widely used "protected groups." The latter term leads to the misconception that EEO laws protect only certain groups, such as racial minorities or women. In fact, EEO laws prohibit making hiring decisions that are based on certain characteristics, such as race and gender, that are irrelevant to job performance. EEO laws protect individuals, not groups. Thus, it is equally illegal under EEO law (but not equally likely) to discriminate against a white male applicant based on his race or gender as it is to do so against an African American female applicant.

The second point is that EEO laws only prohibit employment decisions that are based on these targeted characteristics. Decisions based on other equally irrelevant characteristics may be perfectly acceptable from a legal point of view but wholly contrary to a performance-based approach to hiring. Thus, although the legal perspective probably weeds out some of the worst bases for hiring, *EEO laws do not require that employers use sound, job-related hiring procedures* (unless the procedures create adverse impact, which we describe shortly). That is why the legal perspective needs to be complemented by the performance perspective.

What Is "Discrimination"?

Fundamentally, to discriminate means to make distinctions among people. Discrimination on the basis of performance is the whole point of effective hiring: to make distinctions among applicants in order to hire those who will be most effective. From a legal perspective, however, the term "discrimination" implies making distinctions on the basis of protected characteristics that have no relationship to job performance.

There are two categories of illegal discrimination, which are referred to as disparate (unequal) treatment and disparate impact. It is important to review the hiring process to make sure neither form of discrimination occurs.

Disparate Treatment

The most obvious form of discrimination, disparate treatment involves treating people differently on the basis of age, sex, skin color, and other such protected characteristics. Examples of disparate treatment include

- Asking only women about their ability to meet attendance requirements or about their long-term commitment to an academic career. If regular attendance is essential it may be appropriate to ask applicants about their ability to regularly be at work on time. But asking this only of female applicants is illegal because it treats them differently than male applicants, who may also have problems with regular attendance.
- Not hiring older job applicants because you're concerned they won't learn as quickly as younger applicants. If ability to learn quickly is really essential, you should assess this in all applicants rather than assume that younger applicants are better in that regard. Excluding older workers may also reduce the overall performance of your department by lessening the job-related experience of your staff.
- Requiring applicants with obvious disabilities to have a medical examination, or asking them how their disability would affect their job performance. If physical ability is important, all applicants should have a job-related medical evaluation (which must occur *after* a job offer has been extended).
- Asking only "foreign-looking" applicants or those with "foreign-sounding" names to prove they are eligible to work in the United States. This represents discrimination on the basis of national origin. The Immigration Reform and Control Act requires employers to verify *all* applicants' eligibility to work, but it also prohibits discriminating against noncitizens who are eligible to work in the United States.

Disparate treatment is relatively obvious and is usually considered to be intentional, although the underlying motive is not necessarily malicious. In fact, disparate treatment can occur with the best of misguided intentions. For example, one employer took pains to explain to a female applicant that she would be working in a male-dominated group and asked her whether she felt she could be productive in such an environment. The woman sued, arguing that she was being treated differently than male applicants and that the interviewer's motive was to discourage her from applying for the job. Although that may not have been the interviewer's true motive, he exposed his company to a lawsuit by treating the applicant differently due to her gender.

Disparate Impact

Not all instances of discrimination involve the "smoking gun" that usually characterizes disparate treatment. Disparate impact (also known as adverse impact) includes discrimination that is a consequence—either intentional or unintentional—of a "facially neutral" hiring procedure. A common example is the "good old boy" network in which white male faculty hire other white males they know from a select group of universities. Although there may not have been any intent to exclude women faculty or faculty of color, the relevant issue is that such exclusion was the *consequence* of the recruiting method.

Accommodation of Disabilities

For the most part, the concepts of discrimination we have described to this point apply to all EEO laws. But there is one law, the Americans with Disabilities Act (ADA), that is sufficiently unique to cover separately. The coverage of the ADA is extensive, with a definition of disability that may include as many as forty-three million Americans under its protection. The ADA not only prohibits discrimination, but requires *reasonable accommodation* for individuals who are otherwise qualified to perform a job.

The Americans with Disabilities Act extends the protections of earlier EEO legislation to employees with physical or mental disabilities. Congress defined disabilities broadly as any "physical or mental impairment that substantially limits one or more of the major life activities of an individual." Although recent court decisions have restricted the range of covered disabilities somewhat, it's important to remember that the ADA includes more than such "obvious" disabilities as being blind, deaf, or paralyzed. Rather than trying to describe all the covered conditions, it is probably most useful to remember one fundamental principle that applies not only to disabilities but to all aspects of employment: people who can do the essential duties included in a job should not be held back from doing so by irrelevant factors, whether during hiring or when working at the job.

The ADA acknowledges that a person who has experienced a disability may need adjustments in *how* the essential duties of a job are performed, what the law refers to as "reasonable accommodation." Colleges and universities, in their roles as employers, are responsible for making these accommodations as long as the cost of doing so does not impose an unreasonable burden and safety is not compromised. The Job Accommodation Network [http://janweb.icdi.wvu.edu/kinder/jan.htm] provides extensive information and assistance for working with employees with disabilities.

WHAT HAPPENS IF SOMEONE FILES A DISCRIMINATION COMPLAINT?

If you use a systematic approach for identifying critical performance, treat applicants fairly, and make hiring decisions based on job-relevant performance factors, the chances of being sued for discrimination during hiring are not high. Disparate impact cases in particular appear to be on the decline, and the majority of lawsuits pertain more to unfair treatment of job incumbents (for example, cases of sexual harassment, age discrimination, or gender inequity in pay) rather than of job applicants (Rose, 1993). Nevertheless, lawsuits and complaints do occur, and even unsubstantiated charges can be unnerving. As attorneys say, you can be sued by almost anyone for almost anything. The real issue is whether the person suing can convince a jury—or an investigative reporter—that the complaint has merit.

In this section we provide a brief, informal description of how a *plaintiff,* the person making the complaint, files a charge of discrimination, and what your institution, the *defendant,* can do to defend against the complaint. This will help you understand the process so that you can make hiring decisions that are likely to both reduce the likelihood of such a challenge and stand up to a challenge if one is raised. (If you are currently facing or anticipating a discrimination claim, our treatment of the topic will not suffice. You need to consult legal counsel immediately.)

The Plaintiff's Burden of Proof

Normally, applicants who feel they have been treated unfairly will contact a state Fair Employment Practices Commission, the federal Equal Employment Opportunity Commission, or a plaintiff's attorney. The agency or attorney investigates the case, and as a first step looks to see whether the plaintiff can establish what is called a *prima facie* case. Prima facie evidence is tentative evidence of discrimination, what one might call "reasonable suspicion." The purpose of prima facie evidence is to show that a case is strong enough to require the employer to defend its actions, much as a prosecutor in a criminal case needs to develop an adequate case before a defendant is indicted.

For *disparate treatment* cases, the U.S. Supreme Court outlined the basic elements of prima facie evidence in *McDonnell-Douglas* v. *Green.* Plaintiffs must show that they

- Are protected by a relevant EEO statute

- Applied for a job for which they were qualified

- Were not hired, and the job subsequently remained open to applicants with qualifications similar to their own

More generally, plaintiffs making a disparate treatment case must show that they were treated differently because of their race, national origin, gender, or other protected characteristic.

For *disparate impact* cases, plaintiffs usually establish a prima facie case through the use of statistics. One type of statistic involves showing that the number of *employees* belonging to one group is not proportional to the number of qualified workers of that group in the relevant labor pool. For example, one employer's workforce included less than 1 percent African American workers, whereas the local labor market was 30 percent African American (*United States* v. *Hayes International Corporation,* 1972).

This raised sufficiently serious questions about possible discrimination to require the firm to defend its hiring practices.

Another type of statistic used to establish a prima facie case of disparate impact compares the hiring rate for *applicants* of different groups. If the "pass rate" for one group is less than 80 percent of the pass rate for the majority group, reasonable suspicion exists that the hiring practice may be discriminatory. (See Exhibit 4.2 for an example.)

It is important to remember that prima facie evidence is not proof of discrimination; it simply provides a sufficient basis to compel an employer to respond to the charges. Schools that practice performance-oriented, nondiscriminatory hiring should be able to show that their hiring practices are in fact legitimate and that illegal discrimination did not take place.

Defense of Hiring Practices

The type of evidence needed to defend challenged hiring practices depends on whether the plaintiff has filed a disparate treatment or disparate impact claim. For *disparate treatment* cases defendants must provide a sound nondiscriminatory rationale for not hiring the plaintiff. This might involve showing that the person was not actually qualified for the job, or that the person who was hired was more qualified than the plaintiff. The more compelling the case, the better. The plaintiff is likely to challenge the explanation as being a pretext and that the actual motive was discriminatory. The best defense is a good set of records, compiled at the time of the hire, that documents the reasoning behind hiring decisions and shows that the particular hiring decision was consistent with an overall orientation to performance-based, nondiscriminatory hiring.

Defending against a *disparate impact* charge can be more difficult, because the prima facie case will have already established that a pattern of hiring exists in which people with protected characteristics are hired significantly less frequently. When this is the case, employers need to prove that their hiring procedures are justifiable despite the disparate impact they create against a particular group. The law requires that procedures resulting in disparate impact must be job-related and consistent with business necessity in order to be justifiable. Unlike with disparate treatment,

Exhibit 4.2. Calculating Disparate Impact.

In a typical year, the Facilities Management Department of Metro U. hires roughly 200 maintenance and custodial staff. In reviewing the last year, the department found the following hiring trends for different racial groups:

Racial Group	Number of Applicants	Number Hired	Pass Rate
White	300	120	40%
Latino	120	30	25%
African-American	100	10	10%
Asian-American	80	40	50%

The department obviously hires far fewer African-Americans than applicants of other races, in both absolute and percentage terms. They hire nearly as many Latinos as applicants of Asian descent, though the pass *rates* for the two groups are quite different. Notice also that the pass rate for white applicants is lower than that of Asian-Americans, though far more white applicants are hired than applicants of any other group. Is there evidence of adverse impact, and if so, against whom?

A rule of thumb known as the "Four-fifths Rule" can be used to estimate whether disparate impact exists. The Four-fifths Rule indicates that disparate impact exists if the pass rate for any racial, ethnic, or sex subgroup is less than four-fifths (or 80 percent) of the pass rate of the group with *highest* pass rate. In this example, the group with the highest pass rate is Asian-Americans (with a pass rate of 50 percent). Any group with a pass rate of less than 40 percent (four-fifths of 50 percent) would be experiencing adverse impact; this includes African-American and Latino, but not White applicants. The Facilities Management department would be wise to explore why this level of disparate impact is occurring to ensure that it is not based on discriminatory factors.

there is an obligation to show proof—statistical evidence—to support the argument that the hiring procedures are job-related and of business necessity. This can be done by

• Validating the selection procedures. This requires empirical evidence that differences among applicants on the challenged hiring procedures are actually related to corresponding differences in job performance. Validation is a complex process that depends either on in-house expertise or reliance on a consultant who specializes in the process (see Rosse & Levin [1997] for an overview of validation in the hiring process).

• Establishing that the practice is of business necessity, or "that which is reasonably necessary to the safe and efficient operation of the business" (Sovereign, 1994). Courts have frequently rejected business necessity claims that are not well substantiated with hard evidence. Subjective opinions about what is necessary, or blindly following "best practices," usually are insufficient. Nor are the biases of customers or coworkers. To return to the case of Kwan, the instructor whose "foreign accent" was not accepted by students, the courts have ruled that customer preferences are not in themselves justification for discriminatory hiring decisions. Being understandable is clearly a performance-related requirement for a classroom instructor, but an accent that simply takes getting used to is neither a legal nor a performance basis for not hiring a qualified individual.

Defending against an employment discrimination charge is unpleasant and time-consuming. But before fixating on the legalities of hiring, it's worth reiterating a few key points.

• The risks involved with making hiring decisions are probably lower than most decisions an academic administrator makes, and they can be managed effectively.

• A challenge to hiring procedures—even one that is supported by the EEOC—does not necessarily indicate wrongdoing.

• A performance-based hiring system that has been shown to be job related and applied consistently to all applicants minimizes the

likelihood of a challenge and maximizes the likelihood of successfully defending hiring decisions that are challenged.

- Your primary focus when hiring should be selecting effective
employees.

AFFIRMATIVE ACTION

Affirmative action is perhaps the best example of an employment issue in
which the ethical, performance, and legal perspectives don't always con-
verge easily. Consider, for example, the opening case of Barbara, the
woman who had been hired as dean instead of an internal male candidate
who felt he was equally qualified for the position. Depending on your perspective, this may be viewed as a socially responsible hiring decision or a
case of so-called "reverse discrimination." Deciding on the "right" course
of action is often difficult, especially given the uncertain legal standing of
affirmative action as this book was being written.

From a legal perspective it's important to distinguish between *pure
affirmative action* programs that are limited to efforts to expand the number of underrepresented applicants being considered, and those programs that involve using race or gender as a factor in making a hiring
decision. Efforts to expand the diversity of an applicant pool create little
legal controversy and should form the foundation of institutions' EEO
and diversity programs. A federal district court recently ruled that such
enhanced recruiting could even be encouraged through the use of university incentives, as long as the incentives did not lead to hiring candidates on the basis of race (*Honadle* v. *University of Vermont,* 56 F. Supp.
2d 419, D.Vt., 1999).

Hiring that is based in part on a protected characteristic such as race
or gender is much more controversial and is potentially illegal. The legal
status of race- or gender-conscious hiring is muddled by a patchwork of
decisions by state courts and federal district and circuit courts, most of
which apply to student admission rather than employment decisions. At
the time of this writing, the U.S. Supreme Court had not provided
specific advice regarding affirmative action in higher education since the
early Bakke case (*Regents of the University of California* v. *Bakke,* 438 U.S.

265, 1978). Thus, our summary is based primarily on recent lower-court decisions dealing with challenges to affirmative action plans used for student admissions.

In the Bakke case, the Supreme Court concluded that race could be used as *one* factor in making admission decisions, but that the use of quotas or set-aside programs is unconstitutional. Some legal experts have interpreted this decision to suggest that, particularly for state institutions that must abide by the Fourteenth Amendment's Equal Protection clause, race or gender-conscious treatment can only be justified when there is evidence of prior discrimination (Kaplin & Lee, 1995). Few institutions want to open the Pandora's box of admitting to prior discrimination, and those that do must take pains both to document the prior discrimination and to show that race- or gender-conscious hiring is a reasonable solution (Springer, 2002).

Proponents of affirmative action have argued that another rationale for race- or gender-conscious hiring is that diversity itself can be a relevant performance attribute. For example, the college in our example might argue that Barbara, as a woman, will bring a different perspective to college decisions, as well as provide a role model for female faculty and students. This defense was suggested by Justice Powell's opinion in the *Bakke* case that racial diversity contributes to the "robust exchange of ideas" that is so important in an institution of higher education.

However, a recent series of lower court decisions has questioned the validity of the diversity argument in admissions, as well as how it should be applied. The Supreme Court's refusal to review the *Hopwood* decision (which rejected the University of Texas' diversity-based defense) has been interpreted by some legal scholars to indicate that the current Supreme Court no longer accepts the diversity argument. Yet other recent court decisions—particularly the Sixth Circuit's decision in May 2002 concerning the University of Michigan's use of diversity in admission decisions—have indicated that diversity is a compelling interest of the university. And the issue has been rendered moot by legislation in California, Washington, and Florida that restricts the use of race or gender as admission criteria (Kaplin & Lee, 1995; Schmidt, 1997, 1998; Schneider, 1999; Springer, 2002).

Adding to the uncertainty is the question of how these decisions affect *employment* (rather than student admission) decisions in higher education. The Supreme Court established in *Weber* (*Weber* v. *Kaiser Aluminum Co.,* 443 U.S. 193, 1979) that preferential treatment could be an acceptable remedy for past discrimination in training programs, but only as long as the special programs were temporary, limited in scope, and justified by a history of racial imbalance. Whether the court still accepts this argument since rejecting contractor set-aside programs for minority contractors (*Adarand Constructors, Inc.* v. *Pena, Secretary of Transportation,* 515 U.S. 200, 1995) is an open question.

It's also not certain whether race and gender-conscious hiring can be justified by a diversity argument. In a 1996 case, the Nevada Supreme Court ruled that state universities have a compelling interest in hiring a culturally and ethnically diverse faculty, a decision that the U.S. Supreme Court declined to review. At about the same time, the Third Circuit Court held that diversity could not be used as a factor in making layoff decisions (*Piscataway* v. *Taxman,* 91 F.3d 1547, 3d Cir. 1996), a decision that was settled by the parties involved prior to Supreme Court review.

Given the uncertainty of the legal environment, one approach for enhancing the scope and diversity of your workforce may be to devote far more resources than has been customary in even the recent past to broadening your recruiting efforts in order to attract the most capable candidates of both genders and all ethnicities, ages, and levels of disability. Hiring can then be based on selecting the applicants who best match the profile of capabilities identified in your performance foundation. If diversity is included among these capabilities, you need to be prepared to explain why, as well as to demonstrate convincingly that it was only one of the relevant factors used in your decision.

SUMMARY

A key principle is that performance-based hiring practices are generally also legal and ethical. Note that the converse is not necessarily true: there are plenty of hiring practices that are completely legal but ineffective. The essence of the approach described in this book is to make hiring decisions in a thoughtful, performance-oriented, and systematic manner that treats all applicants fairly. The critical issues from the perspectives of performance-based hiring as well as legal, moral, and ethical compliance are to

- Understand the nature of the job and what employee attributes are necessary for the safe and effective conduct of the work by using the procedures described in Chapter Two.

- Base your hiring decisions solely on these job-related applicant attributes, not on irrelevant and possibly illegal factors.

- Use hiring tools that have been shown to validly measure these attributes.

- Evaluate your hiring procedures for disparate impact (disproportionate rejection of applicants with certain characteristics, such as race or gender). If evidence of disparate impact is found, determine whether the hiring procedure is job-related and whether there are other, equally effective procedures that produce less disparate impact.

- Monitor your hiring (and other employment) procedures to ensure that all applicants are treated consistently, with the important exception that applicants with disabilities receive whatever accommodations are reasonable and necessary to allow them to be evaluated fairly on the basis of their ability to perform the job.

- Document your hiring (and other personnel) decisions. Following systematic and effective decision-making principles presented in Chapter Six will aid in documenting your decisions, and such documentation will help you establish, if necessary, that you had a legitimate rationale for every decision.

PART III

The Hiring Decision

5

Evaluating Applicants

I N THIS chapter you will identify a set of assessment procedures—such as application materials, interviews, reference checks, and work samples—that can comprehensively and accurately measure the performance attributes essential for success on the job. These attributes were identified in the performance foundation you created in Chapter Two. In that chapter we described how to identify the knowledge, skills, abilities, and the Fit and Risk Factors associated with successful performance. If by chance you've opened the book directly to this chapter, we strongly encourage you to work through Chapter Two before proceeding in this chapter to develop a Performance Attributes Matrix (PAM) of hiring methods.

THE PERFORMANCE ATTRIBUTES MATRIX AND CHOOSING TOOLS FOR YOUR HIRING SYSTEM

A Performance Attribute Matrix begins with the critical knowledge, skills, abilities, and other attributes (KSOAs) you identified in the performance foundation for the job. These attributes are listed in the rows of a matrix, or spreadsheet, and the various hiring tools you might use to assess the attributes are included in the columns of the matrix. You then fill in the matrix with Xs to indicate which hiring tools will be used to measure each attribute. An example for the job of residence hall advisor is shown in Exhibit 5.1.

Although this approach may seem unfamiliar, there are a number of reasons to use a Performance Attribute Matrix rather than less structured, more ad hoc approaches to choosing and using hiring tools:

- The matrix provides a simple, visual representation of complex information that makes it easy to ensure that you've not forgotten to measure any of the critical attributes you previously identified. Without a matrix, it's easy to focus all your attention on one attribute and then forget to measure others that you identified as important.

- The matrix organizes the process of selecting hiring tools around their real purpose—assessing applicants' job-relevant attributes—rather than irrelevant factors such as your biases regarding different tools.

- The matrix reminds you that there may be multiple ways of assessing a particular attribute. For example, Exhibit 5.1 suggests that problem-solving skills might be assessed in a behavioral interview, by ratings from former employers, or through a role play in which the applicant is challenged to solve a problem that might arise on the job. Some of the potential methods shown in the preliminary matrix may be ruled out as you proceed (for example, simulations may be too costly in some circumstances), in which case the matrix provides you with a guide of effective alternatives. The matrix also shows you where multiple methods can be used to get more reliable information.

Exhibit 5.1. Performance Attributes Matrix for Residence Hall Advisor.

Attribute	Application/ Vita	Interview	Reference Checks	Work Sample	Employment Test	Integrity Test
Oral Communication		X	X			
Written Communication	X			X		
Empathetic Listening		X	X			
Problem Solving		X	X	X		
Honesty/Integrity		X	X			X
Safety Orientation		X	X		X	

- The matrix discourages you from trying to assess too many attributes with one hiring tool. For example, typical searches are almost entirely centered around interviews, a tactic that is both inefficient and likely to lead to serious errors.

Types of Assessments to Include in Your Matrix

What are the various possible ways of measuring differences in applicants' skills, knowledge, abilities, and other job-relevant characteristics? The ideal approach might be to observe applicants actually performing the job for which they are being hired. A more practical variation of this approach is to create a simulated work environment in which applicants demonstrate the critical tasks. This is the essence of *work samples,* which we discuss in more detail later in this chapter. Work samples are most appropriate when your goal is to measure *developed skills* among experienced employees.

If time or cost constraints make it impossible to observe directly performance on a task, an alternative is to ask others who have observed the applicant to rate the person's performance. If you're hiring internally, *prior performance appraisal* information may be useful if it's accurate and relevant to the job the person is applying for. More generally, checking *references* can be a source of information about applicants' skills, as well as their characteristic approach to work and coworkers.

Another approach is to assess an applicant's relevant experience, knowledge, or training. This approach is less direct than measuring skills, since it assumes that the applicant can translate the experience into effective job performance. In some cases, you can assess experience, knowledge, and training by asking appropriate questions on an *application form,* with narrative *accomplishment records,* or by reviewing a vita or résumé. *Job knowledge tests* can provide a more thorough and standardized assessment of understanding of critical information.

Abilities and personality traits are the most general—and least observable—attributes of applicants. Abilities are particularly relevant when hiring applicants who do not have experience doing the kind of work you're hiring for or when the nature of the work is changing rapidly. Since you're looking for a person's potential, rather than their past accomplishments, it's difficult to use the kind of assessment approaches we've discussed so far. For that reason, abilities are often measured by *standardized tests* designed to assess basic mental or physical abilities. Personality and so-called "behavioral" tests can be used to evaluate typical ways of behaving, and may also be used to predict dishonesty or other problem behaviors. As a general rule, tests have the advantage of being reliable and easily quantified, though some kinds of tests may raise issues of invasion of privacy or unfair discrimination.

Evaluation of Assessment Tools

Your choice of a general category of hiring tool—as well as a specific tool within that category—should be based on four criteria: accuracy, practicality, fairness, and legality. In the following pages we provide a brief overview of these technical criteria; readers interested in a somewhat more extended discussion may wish to read *High-Impact Hiring* (Rosse & Levin, 1997), while those interested in a considerably more technical discussion are referred to Gatewood and Feild's *Human Resource Selection* (Gatewood & Feild, 2000).

Accuracy

The most obvious standard for evaluating hiring tools is *accuracy,* or how well the procedure actually measures the job-related attributes you're looking for in applicants. From a technical perspective, accuracy is actually a function of two concepts, *reliability* and *validity.* Saying that a measure is reliable can mean many things in different contexts and for different people. In the context of evaluating hiring tools, a reliable measure has three characteristics.

• Measurements based on a reliable measure are stable over time and under different conditions (*test-retest reliability*). For example, if you were to use a test to screen applicants, you would expect that the applicants' scores would not vary if they took the test this Tuesday or next Thursday.

• Measurements on a reliable measure will agree with measurements on other reliable tools intended to measure the same thing. For example, if you used two forms of an employment test to reduce cheating, you would expect scores on the two versions of the test to be comparable (*parallel forms reliability*). Or if two interviewers compare notes on an interview they both attended, you would like to see considerable agreement (*inter-rater reliability*). One advantage of the structured interviewing approach described later in this chapter is that it increases interrater reliability.

• All parts of a measuring tool should be consistent at measuring the same attribute (*internal consistency*). For example, if an employment test was intended only to measure mathematical skills, you would not want scores to be affected by applicants' ability to comprehend complex word problems.

Reliability is the first standard for accuracy because measures that are not reliable have a difficult time meeting the second standard for accuracy: validity. Validity is another word that has many lay meanings, but for our purposes validity may be defined as the accuracy of the inferences that we draw from a measure. For example, from the glowing praise lavished upon a candidate by a former department head we might draw the inference that the individual will make a fine employee. Unfortunately, such an inference is not always correct. In contrast, by asking candidates to perform a sample of the work they would actually perform on the job, we might draw the inference that those who perform acceptably on the work sample are more likely to perform well on the job. That inference is more often correct.

Validity (and the process of validating hiring tools) is more complex and technical than reliability. Validation is the process of verifying the inferences we draw, using either empirical or logical means. Empirical (or criterion-related) validation involves statistical analyses of the correlation between a hiring tool and some measure(s) of job performance; for example, showing that applicants who score higher on a structured job interview turn out to be higher performers than applicants with lower interview scores. Logical (content or construct) validation is done by showing a clear and convincing overlap between the requirements of a job and the content of a hiring tool. For example, you might validate your reference-checking procedures by showing that the questions you ask directly tap the attributes you identified in the performance foundation for the job.

Good estimates of validity and reliability exist for different categories of hiring tools and are summarized in Exhibit 5.2. Once you've identified procedures that have acceptable accuracy, your final choice among accurate procedures is likely to be based on the additional criteria of practicality, perceived fairness, and legal acceptability.

Practicality

There's not much point in using even a valid hiring tool if the resources required to use the tool exceed the benefits it provides, particularly if an alternative exists that has higher validity or delivers equivalent validity while requiring fewer resources. The primary costs for most hiring procedures involve labor (such as staff time to administer tests and professional time involved in conducting interviews, work samples, and reference checks). Decisions to include more interviewers, or more observers of a work sample, can increase some of these costs. Costs can also include direct material or licensing costs, as with standardized tests. (Note that we are not including overall costs involved in the search process or in recruiting).

In assessing practicality, the key issue is to consider the overall cost-effectiveness (and ease of implementation) of alternative tools rather than focusing exclusively on absolute costs. Costs and other factors affecting practicality are more situation-dependent than are estimates of accuracy. Therefore, the ratings of practicality in Exhibit 5.2 should be viewed simply as a starting point for your own assessment of cost-effectiveness.

Perceived Fairness

Another important, and often overlooked, consideration is how applicants react to the hiring process. Selection procedures that applicants view as unfair, irrelevant, or invasive of their privacy may cause your carefully recruited and screened applicants to decide to reject your institution just when you've decided to accept them. Leaving applicants with a bad impression can be particularly costly in close-knit professional circles and in smaller college towns where the word gets around quickly.

Exhibit 5.2. Comparison of Hiring Tools.

	Reliability	Validity	Practicality	Acceptability	Disparate Impact
Background					
Résumés	Moderate	Low	High	High?	Low-Moderate
References	Low	Moderate	Moderate	Moderate	Low-Moderate
Applications	Moderate	Low-Moderate	High	Moderate-High?	Moderate
Biodata	High	Moderate-High	Moderate	Moderate?	Low-Moderate
Interviews					
Unstructured	Low	Low-Moderate	Moderate	High	Moderate-High
Structured	High	High	Moderate	Moderate-High?	Low?
Tests					
Ability	High	High	Moderate	Low-Moderate?	High
Job Knowledge	High	High	Moderate-High	High?	Low
Personality	Moderate	Moderate	Moderate	Low-Moderate	Low
Interest	High	Low	Moderate	Moderate?	Low
Integrity	High	High	Moderate	Low-Moderate	Low
Drug*	High	Moderate-High	Low-Moderate	Low-Moderate	Low
Performance	High	High	Moderate	High	Low

Notes:
Evaluations are general summaries for each category. Different measures within each category may vary substantially. "?" indicates that research is inconclusive.
* Evaluations of reliability and validity are based on confirmatory tests.
Source: Adapted from Rosse & Levin (1997)

In general, applicants react more positively to procedures that appear to be job-related. Work samples and job knowledge tests, for example, are generally well received because they so clearly resemble the nature of the job being applied for. More abstract tests of mental ability are less obviously related to job performance, and personality inventories may bear little or no obvious relationship to job requirements. (Note, however, that we are talking only about the applicants' *perceptions* of job relatedness. Personality and general ability tests are often effective at predicting job performance without this being obvious to job applicants or other casual observers.)

A second important factor in applicants' reactions to hiring tools is privacy. A number of selection procedures—such as integrity (honesty) tests, drug screening, and personality assessments—may be viewed by many job applicants as an unwarranted invasion of their privacy, unless their use is carefully explained. This is especially likely for faculty and administrative positions, where there is little tradition of standardized testing as part of the hiring process.

Another factor that affects applicants' attitudes toward a selection system is how *systematic* it appears to be. A systematic hiring approach communicates that an institution is serious about hiring good employees; applicants who "survive" such a rigorous selection process feel justifiably proud about being part of a company with high standards (Rosse, Miller, & Stecher, 1994).

Legality

We have left our discussion of legal criteria for last because we believe that legal considerations are largely subsumed in the other criteria, particularly the criterion of accuracy. As you read in Chapter Four, a primary legal obligation is to make hiring decisions without regard to protected personal characteristics such as age, race, religion, gender, or disability. By developing a Performance Attributes Matrix based on a rigorous performance foundation, you have virtually assured that your hiring decisions are based on job-relevant factors rather than discriminatory ones. (And the matrix provides very effective documentation of this.)

Another legal obligation is to monitor the hiring process to ensure that all applicants are treated similarly (with the exception of making reasonable accommodations for applicants with disabilities) and determine whether the hiring procedures create disparate impact against groups of individuals with protected characteristics. If disparate impact does occur, and you are challenged, you will need to show the job-relatedness (validity) of the practice causing the disparate impact.

Each of these standards—accuracy, practicality, fairness, and legality—should be applied as you decide what assessment tools to include in your Performance Attributes Matrix. As you decide on assessments, it can also be helpful to categorize them in terms of three basic steps in evaluating applicants: *initial screening* (involving application forms, vitae or résumés, and cover letters), *evaluation* (incorporating interviews, work samples, and perhaps tests), and *finalist review.*

INITIAL SCREENING OF APPLICANTS

Once the recruiting campaign is under way, you will begin to receive applications from interested individuals. Sometimes this flow will be only a trickle, but often it will escalate into a flood of applicants, many of whom are not even remotely qualified for the position. Thus, the primary purpose of assessments used in the screening stage is to quickly and accurately eliminate the clearly unqualified. There is usually a strong temptation to use this stage to identify outstanding candidates. This is a reasonable goal, but it should be secondary to your primary mission of winnowing the applicant pool down to a size that can be systematically evaluated against your hiring standards. As you will learn in the next chapter, your hiring decisions are improved by first making sure that applicants who are unacceptable on one or more critical performance criteria are removed from consideration. Once you have accomplished that, you can move on to identify a first cut of five to twenty high-potential people, the specific number being dependent on how successful your recruitment efforts have been. You can then use the other assessment tools in this chapter to winnow your semifinalists to a pool of three (or so) finalists.

Often the search committee chair or an administrative assistant does the initial screening as the applications arrive. For searches that generate a smaller applicant pool this may be reasonable, but screening can quickly become a significant burden. When search committees are used, it may make sense to delegate the responsibility for this prescreening to a sub-committee who can divide up the task. In any case, it is important that the person(s) doing the prescreening understand fully the requirements for the job and the legitimate bases for eliminating applicants at this first hurdle.

Depending on the nature of the job, the basic material on which to make initial screening decisions is typically either an application form (with or without a cover letter) or a vita (usually accompanied by a cover letter). Well-designed application forms are structured so that you can quickly determine whether or not an applicant meets the basic requirements for a job. Unfortunately, the majority of application forms are designed more for record-keeping than for evaluating qualifications, so you are probably going to need to collect additional information before you can begin to effectively screen applicants. One way to accomplish this is to specify in your recruiting materials that applicants should provide a cover letter that describes their qualifications with specific reference to the *critical attributes* you wish to assess in the application materials. To reduce tendencies toward inflated self-descriptions, ask candidates to provide specific examples of how their experience and training demonstrate their qualifications for the positions. Such *accomplishment records* have a good track record for providing valid information, as long as the writing skills required to craft the summary statements don't exceed the requirements of the job itself (Hough, 1984).

A similar approach makes sense for jobs that traditionally require submissions of vitae rather than application forms. Unlike application forms, cover letters and vitae allow applicants considerable leeway to present (or omit) what information they wish. Some of the information may be irrelevant, and it may be less obvious what critical information is missing. One way to efficiently evaluate vitae, résumés, or cover letters is to highlight (for example, with a highlighting marker or pencil) key terms that match up with the attributes you identified as critical for the position, a "low-tech" version of recruiting software that scans resumes for key terms.

Another approach is to create a summary qualifications sheet for each applicant that lists the critical attributes that you expect to be able to evaluate from an application letter or vita. Chapter Six provides a decision-making table (Exhibit 6.2) that is particularly relevant for deciding among finalists but that can be modified for screening purposes. To do so, list the critical attributes for the job in columns across the top of the table or spreadsheet, and list the names of the applicants down the side. For each applicant, place a check-mark in the corresponding space when their application materials demonstrate a level of qualification that is at least acceptable for that critical attribute. Place an X where that level of qualification is unacceptable. Leave the space blank where the level of qualification can't be assessed. Applicants who lack critical qualifications are rejected, those with at least acceptable levels continue on, and you can note areas where you will need to assess at a later stage whether qualifications are at least acceptable.

With this approach, you do not spend time or resources trying to formally identify highly desirable candidates during the initial screening process. This has three advantages. First, the process moves more quickly. Second, you reduce the likelihood of phenomena such as premature closure and first-impression bias. You might informally note candidates you are particularly impressed with, but you are less likely to skew your thought process or the committee's decision process toward them. Third, you increase the validity of the system because you postpone making these more refined assessments until you have a greater amount of more valid information.

Here are a few additional points to keep in mind when developing your screening strategy:

- Your PAM will probably include only a limited number of attributes that can reasonably be evaluated during the initial screening process. Don't try to evaluate attributes that aren't appropriately assessed in the application materials (interpersonal skills, for example), but also don't forget to include these evaluations in later stages of the hiring process.
- Applicants who are lacking critical qualifications will be eliminated at this stage, so be sure that you are making this first cut only on the basis of critical (not optional, or desirable) attributes.
- Application forms are notorious for including questions that are not job-related and that may invite legal challenge. This is particularly true of

generic or universal application forms intended to be used for many types of jobs. If you choose not to develop a customized application form that can be reviewed in advance for compliance, consider developing a written protocol that explicitly indicates how material in the application form was used (and, if necessary, states that irrelevant information was *not* included in your evaluations).

• It's important to keep applicants informed about the progress of your search. Applicants who are eliminated during the prescreening should promptly be sent a "thank you for applying" letter, and similar letters should go to those who are eliminated at later steps. It's also important to keep finalists informed of their status, particularly when you are ready to begin checking references. To help manage this process, it's a good idea to create a tracking system as you begin to receive applications. This can be as simple as a spreadsheet that lists each applicant's name and has a column for each step in the review process; placing a check in the appropriate column is a good way of making sure that nothing has been overlooked.

IN-DEPTH EVALUATION OF CANDIDATES

The goal of the initial screening process is to create a smaller pool of applicants who are worth looking at more carefully. The next step is intended to provide you with both a broader and deeper base of information that will help you distinguish between those who are simply adequate and those who are your preferred candidates (as well as continue to eliminate applicants who are unqualified). In this section we begin by discussing the two most common assessment procedures, interviews and work samples, and also mention the possibility of using standardized tests. We end the chapter with a discussion of the importance of reference checks.

Interviews

Interviews are the one universal of hiring; it's hard to imagine a situation in which a person is hired for a job without going through at least one employment interview. Interviews may be conducted face-to-face, by phone, or even by videoconference. They may be one-on-one, or they may be conducted as a panel interview. Interviews are as varied as they are ubiquitous. Yet all too often interviews are of limited value—and sometimes even detrimental—to effective hiring.

Volumes of research on employment interviews have been written, and we will not attempt to replicate that literature here. The take-home message is that ad hoc interviews generally lack reliability (particularly in terms of interrater agreement), provide limited valid information about applicants, are subject to a wide variety of biases, and are a common target of litigation (Arvey & Campion, 1982; McDaniel, Whetzel, Schmidt, & Maurer, 1994). The good news is that structured, job-related interviews can overcome these problems and be an integral part of a performance-based hiring approach.

Interviews Should Remain Job-Related

It should be obvious that interview questions ought to be job-related, yet this is often not the case. Why? One reason is that interviews are often not given the attention by interviewers that they deserve. Too often we treat interviews simply as a conversation without a clear purpose. Certainly the overall purpose is to evaluate the applicant, but how often have we thought carefully in advance of conducting an interview about what qualifications we're looking for and how we can validly assess those qualifications? Failing to do this homework and relying instead on "gut feelings" is an invitation for inaccurate evaluations or those influenced by stereotypes and biases.

Studies show that a host of such biases affect interview ratings. One of the most powerful has to do with attractiveness of the applicant; people just naturally tend to prefer attractive people (and while definitions of "attractiveness" vary, few are likely to be performance-relevant for higher education jobs). A similar bias involves preferences for individuals who are similar to ourselves, whether that similarity is as irrelevant as having the same hobby, or as potentially relevant as having similar research interests. More subtle at times are biases based on racial, gender, age, or other discriminatory stereotypes. But whether conscious or unconscious, legally proscribed or not, biases by definition produce distorted information and lower the quality of hiring decisions.

The solution is straightforward: make sure all of your interview questions are directly related to critical attributes identified in your Performance Attributes Matrix. Use your PAM to determine which attributes should be addressed in the interview, and then make sure that you develop questions *in advance* of the interview that assess these attributes. Ask those questions consistently of all applicants, and resist the temptation to "wing it" with impromptu questions that are not job related. That's not to say that you shouldn't follow up on intuitions that arise during the interview; just make sure that the follow-up questions are clearly related to your performance foundation.

This job-focused approach is also the simplest and most effective way of dealing with the common concern about "what questions can't I ask in interviews"? Although there are some clearly taboo questions (see Exhibit 5.3 for some examples), it can be difficult to memorize a list of forbidden interview topics or the laws underlying them. Asking only job-related questions and treating all applicants equally regardless of protected characteristics virtually assures that your interviews will be legal as well as valid.

Use of Structured Questions

Another aspect of structure concerns *how* you ask interview questions. In addition to avoiding job-irrelevant biases, you also want to make sure that a facile applicant is not misleading you. Asking vague, unverifiable, and predictable questions such as, "Where do you expect to be in five years?" or "What do you think is your greatest weakness?" is likely to result in well-practiced but meaningless answers.

Research identifies two types of structured interviewing techniques with excellent track records for gathering accurate, job-related information from interviewees. Both accomplish this by focusing on actual examples of job-related behavior; their primary difference is that one (Behavior Description Interviewing) asks applicants to describe how they acted in actual situations in the past, whereas the other (Situational Interviewing) asks applicants to describe how they *would* act in hypothetical job situations.

Behavior Description Interviewing is based on the commonsense notion that past behavior is generally a good predictor of future behavior (Janz,

Exhibit 5.3. Potentially Illegal Preemployment Inquiries.

Gender or Race:
- Don't ask unless it's job-related (which is very rare).
- Avoid indirect indicators, such as requesting a photograph, listing of nonrelevant hobbies or social club memberships, and so forth.

Marital/Family Status
- *Prohibited* (this may imply discrimination against women): Asking applicants if they are married, if they have children, or what their child care arrangements are.
- *Allowable:* Asking applicants if they can meet attendance requirements (if asked equally of all applicants)

Age
- Best not to ask, except for minimum age requirements. Also avoid indirect indicators, such as date of graduation from high school.

Religion
- Don't ask any questions that would suggest religious preferences, unless religion is relevant (rarely the case except for some jobs in religiously affiliated institutions).

Criminal Record
- *Prohibited:* Asking questions about prior *arrests* (because they presume guilt and may create adverse impact).
- Questions about relevant convictions are acceptable, but they should be accompanied by a statement that convictions will not necessarily disqualify the applicant and that they will be considered in the context of the seriousness of the crime, how long ago it occurred, and the applicant's subsequent behavior.

Credit History
- Prohibited unless specifically job-related (for example, if the employee would handle money or valuables).

(continued)

Exhibit 5.3. Potentially Illegal Preemployment Inquiries. (continued)

- Fair Credit Reporting Act requires notifying applicants that their credit is being checked. If applicants are turned down due to credit history, applicant must be informed of the name of the credit agency that provided the information.

Disabilities and Health Status
- *Prohibited:* Asking applicants if they have a disability (although you should provide applicants an opportunity to self-identify any disabilities).
  Asking applicants if they will require an accommodation to perform the job.
  Asking applicants about job-related injuries or workers' compensation history.
  Medical examinations *prior* to a job offer.
- *Allowable:* Asking about an applicant's ability to perform specific job functions, or asking applicants to describe or demonstrate how they would perform job tasks—if asked of all applicants.
  Asking applicants if they can meet attendance requirements or about their attendance on past jobs. (However, questions about missing work due to *illness* are prohibited, since this might reveal that a person is disabled.)
  Questions about current or past use of illegal drugs (but not about prior addiction, or about amount of drugs used which might reveal an addiction).
  Asking applicants if they drink alcohol or whether they have been convicted of driving under the influence (but not about alcoholism, which is a covered disability).

Source: Adapted from Rosse & Levin (1997).

1986). Job applicants who can describe specific instances of effective relevant performance on prior jobs are likely to perform similarly in the job for which they're being hired. Although Behavior Description interviews usually include questions that pertain to prior work experience that is either directly or indirectly related to the job being recruited, you may also want to develop alternate questions for applicants who have not had directly relevant work experience.

Consider, for example, a position in which the employee has to interact with students and the ability to constructively and efficiently handle conflict is a critical component. In using a Behavior Description approach, you might ask, "Can you describe for me a situation in which you've been involved in a conflict with someone and had to reach a resolution that the other party initially did not want to accept? What was the situation, and how did it work out?" If the applicant had never worked in a student services area, but had worked in retail sales, you might ask the person to describe a situation in which he or she had to work with a customer who was angry about the quality of a product. Applicants who have never worked in a retail setting might instead be asked to describe how they dealt with a friend who was angry about the applicant not following through on a commitment.

Situational Interviewing develops "what if" questions based on actual job situations that are critical to success (Latham, Saari, Pursell, & Campion, 1980). These incidents are then used to develop hypothetical scenarios that applicants are asked to imagine themselves experiencing; applicants are evaluated on their description of how they would handle the situation. A Situational Interviewing strategy might ask, "One essential part of this job involves collection of overdue payments. Imagine that a student begins yelling at you about how faceless and uncaring the university is, and says that you will have to hire an attorney if you ever want to get the money you claim is owed. How would you respond?"

Because they focus on actual examples of past behavior, Behavior Description questions are presumed to be less vulnerable to faking (making up an answer that the interviewee thinks you want to hear), particularly if you follow up with probing questions that make it more difficult for the interviewees to fabricate the story as they go. Although that makes intuitive sense, studies show that both Behavior Description and Situational Interview questions have validities that are comparable and significantly better than unstructured interviews (McDaniel et al., 1994). This may, however, be less true for high-level positions, such as senior administrators, for which situational interview questions seem to work less well (Huffcutt, Weekley, Wiesner, DeGroot, & Jones, 2001).

Our recommendation is to use a mix of Behavior Description and situational questions in most interviews. A majority of the questions can be of the behavior-description type to focus on the applicant's past success on similar performance requirements. You may then want to add some situational questions both to allow for a change of pace and to see how well applicants can think on their feet, particularly for entry-level applicants who have less directly relevant experience.

A Structured Approach to Scoring Interviews

You can further enhance your interviewing by scoring applicants' answers to the interview questions relative to the attribute being assessed. Giving applicants a separate rating on each attribute allows much more precision than the more common approach of forming an overall, subjective impression of a candidate and then using that "gut reaction" to decide whether to hire the applicant. Deciding in advance how to score interview responses also provides another opportunity to think carefully about what you're looking for in a candidate. This is particularly true if you develop sample answers to guide your ratings, because thinking about appropriate and inappropriate responses focuses attention on the behaviors—rather than vague traits—that are essential to job performance.

Developing rating scales isn't a complicated process. The first requirement is a clear description of what attributes should form the basis for scoring an applicant's answers. In other words, the rating scale should make it clear to anyone who's conducting an interview exactly what constitutes a "good" answer. Without a rating guide, different interviewers may use the same question to evaluate different (and possibly irrelevant) attributes.

The second requirement is some basis for assigning a score to applicants' answers. Some approaches use simple rating scales with adjectives such as *excellent, good, fair,* or *poor.* Others involve rating the applicants' answers relative to those of others, such as in the top, second, middle, fourth, or last 20 percent of all candidates. The optimal strategy is to develop a rating scale based on examples of unacceptable, acceptable, and outstanding answers. With any of these approaches, the rating forms should provide space to include comments, examples, or quotes to support the ratings assigned.

Developing preplanned, job-related, behaviorally focused interview questions and rating scales is the heart of effective interviewing. Once you have built that foundation, you may find it useful to review Exhibit 5.4 for some additional interviewing tips.

Exhibit 5.4. More Interviewing Tips.

- *Make the interviewee comfortable.* Forget anything you may have heard about "stress interviews." Your goal is to create an atmosphere that encourages applicants to be forthcoming and that also makes them want to take the job if you offer it to them. This includes making them feel welcome and at ease during and after the interview and also means giving applicants who are making a campus visit some time to rest, prepare for presentations, and see the campus community.

- *Allow enough time for the interview.* A common mistake is to try to use the interview to assess all the critical attributes, which results in interviews that are rushed, applicants that feel harried, and information that is not valid. Another common mistake is to try to use the interview for too many different purposes; you probably can't assess all the relevant attributes, answer the interviewees' questions, and sell your campus as an ideal employer all in one thirty-minute interview. By the time you put the applicant at ease, ask at least two questions related to each critical attribute that you intend to assess in the interview (along with probes), and close the interview, you will have probably spent an hour or more with the candidate.

(continued)

Exhibit 5.4. More Interviewing Tips. (continued)

- *Let the applicant talk.* Your primary purpose is to learn more about the applicant, and to do this you must let the applicant do most of the talking. If you ask good questions that get the applicant talking about his or her past work-relevant experience, this should be easy. For many of us, the hard parts are listening carefully to assess the applicant's answer and fighting the temptation to interrupt.

- *Evaluate the applicant's strengths and weaknesses on specific attributes, not overall suitability.* Overall impressions are too vulnerable to bias and are often affected by factors that are irrelevant to job performance.

- *Don't make hiring decisions during the interview.* Hiring decisions should be based on a thoughtful analysis of all the information about applicants, not just the information from the interview. (Effective decision making will be discussed in the next chapter.)

- *Practice makes perfect.* To become proficient at interviewing you need to practice the key skills and get feedback on how well you're doing. Plan some time for practice and feedback as part of your next round of interviews. Start by working with your colleagues in developing the structured interview for the position. Then, if there will be several people conducting interviews, practice interviewing each other. If you are the only person doing the interviewing, practice interviewing and getting feedback from a current incumbent of the position (or a similar position).

- *Coordinate with others.* One of the challenges of most academic hiring is the number of people who are involved in the process. Effective coordination involves making sure that all the interviewers agree on the critical attributes to be assessed, that they all follow the guidelines for structured interviewing, and that they reach their initial evaluations independently of one another (particularly if the interviewers will subsequently meet to discuss their evaluations and make a hiring decision). In some cases, you may also want to divide up the interview questions among the interviewers so that the applicant doesn't end up being asked the same question by five different interviewers. Another common way to coordinate multiple interviewers is to use a panel interview, in which the whole search committee simultaneously interviews the applicant, for example. Although panel interviews are often no more valid than individual interviews (McDaniel and others, 1994), they may offer some efficiency advantages.

- *Avoid the appearance of any impropriety.* For many academic positions it is customary to conduct initial screening interviews at academic conferences. Because of a lack of formal interviewing facilities, or in an attempt to save money, these interviews are sometimes conducted in hotel rooms, bars, or other less than ideal locations. At a minimum these contexts can interfere with the professional conduct of the interview; worse, they may also create an atmosphere that suggests or encourages inappropriate conduct. To avoid even the appearance of impropriety, interviews should be conducted in semi-public locations, such as conference areas set aside for job interviews, public hotel areas that provide a business-like context, or offices with open doors.

Work Samples

Work samples involve observation or other evaluation of applicants actually performing the work they are being hired to do, but under controlled conditions. As you read earlier in this chapter, the advantage of work samples is that they provide a relatively direct assessment of relevant behavior, free of many of the inferences that are required when interviewing or evaluating a résumé. As a consequence, work samples tend to result in evaluations that are both valid and readily acceptable to applicants.

An example of a work sample in academic hiring is the "job talk" or research colloquium that faculty candidates are often expected to provide during a campus visit. Presumably, these presentations are intended not only to familiarize people with the candidate's research or creative work but also to allow the candidate to demonstrate expository and reasoning skills. Skill in making presentations is generally an important part of the research endeavor, and such a presentation might even be useful for evaluating classroom teaching skill. Yet it is also easy to see how these kinds of presentations can become a ritual conducted because of tradition rather than to actually predict performance. Analyzing the limitations of research colloquia as work samples will give us a better understanding of how to use work samples more effectively.

One reason that research colloquia may not be effective as selection tools is that they tend to emphasize *maximal* rather than *typical* performance. Conducting such a presentation is a command performance, and candidates know that they must be good to be successful. Maximal performance tests can tell you about the limits of a person's performance but don't necessarily tell you how a person will perform day-to-day. Can job talks predict classroom teaching effectiveness? It's one thing to create a single impressive presentation (particularly one you use for multiple interviews), and something else to create and continuously update a set of thirty or more lectures for a semester-long course.

It's tempting to conclude that *failing* a maximal performance test gives unequivocal evidence that a person *cannot* perform a task successfully. That might be a reasonable conclusion if the test involves multiple assessments of related behaviors under different conditions, but typical "tests" like the research colloquium represent only a single snapshot of performance and under artificially stressful conditions. Even seasoned presenters can have a bad day, particularly when they've had a long flight, an uncomfortable or unfamiliar bed to sleep in, a fatiguing schedule of appointments, and a strong desire to get the job.

A second limitation is that it is possible for the nature of this particular work sample to introduce its own set of biases. How often have we all heard (or uttered) the lament, "We were so blown away by the job talk that we didn't bother to read any of the candidate's papers or check the candidate's references"? This kind of bias can be exacerbated when applicants with a checkered work history put additional effort into their presentation with the hope of creating just that kind of euphoric enthusiasm among the search committee (Levin & Zickar, 2002).

Third, and most fundamentally, job talks sample only a portion of a professor's job. They may provide a good example of research skills, particularly research presentation skills, and a partial sample of teaching skills, but they provide limited insights into student advising skills, ability to mentor graduate students, willingness to contribute to committee work, and so forth. Work samples, as with interviews and other selection procedures, should be one part of a comprehensive assessment system designed to measure all of these skills. Attributes that cannot be assessed in a job talk might be assessed in a different form of work sample or in interviews, reference checks, and so forth.

Other examples of work samples for faculty hiring include published articles or other creative work, observing candidates teach a class during a campus visit, or having them interact with students in a more informal setting to observe their skill in working with and advising students. In a similar fashion, prospective administrators might be asked to develop and present a plan, program, or budget outline relevant to the position. Applicants for technical positions could be asked to provide a sample of their prior work (such as an example of a computer program they've developed) or to conduct a simulated task (such as asking an applicant for a laboratory technician job to demonstrate their proficiency on a particular procedure).

Although work samples take some effort to design and administer, they have a strong track record of validity, little evidence of adverse impact, and are generally well-received by job applicants. The key is to select job-relevant attributes that can be accurately and practically assessed through simulated work activities, administer and evaluate those activities in a uniform and job-relevant fashion, and interpret the resulting information as one component of an overall hiring system.

Employment Testing

One of the ironies of life is that tests, an integral part of academic life, are used far less often for hiring in academia than in most other occupational fields. Could it be that as faculty we are too aware of the limitations of our own tests to trust them for making hiring decisions? Before dismissing testing too quickly, it's instructive to consider a balanced picture of their advantages and disadvantages.

Advantages of Testing

The potential advantages of tests as a means of evaluating job applicants are that they are efficient and standardized. By *efficient,* we refer to two strengths of tests. The first is that tests are one of the least expensive forms of collecting information. They are one of the few hiring procedures that you are likely to purchase rather than develop, but their cost advantage results from the minimal investment in *your* valuable time, compared to the time you invest in developing and then participating in interviews or reference checks.

For example, suppose you are hiring for a technical position in which you want to assess applicants' job-specific knowledge. One way would be to ask applicants to describe what they know during the interview, but that takes time and includes only the finalists who are chosen for interviews. A more efficient alternative might be to have applicants complete a short job knowledge test—for example, of accounting, word processing, computer programming knowledge—and reserve valuable interview time to assess other attributes for which interviews are better suited.

Another potential advantage of tests is that, unlike application cover letters, references, or even interviews, you can be confident that all applicants received the same questions. By using carefully designed tests, you can also be more confident that those questions are both valid and legal.

Disadvantages of Testing

In most cases, the biggest concerns about testing have to do with fairness. For cognitive ability tests, the concern is often about potential racial discrimination or about people who don't "test well." Personality, drug, and integrity (honesty) tests may raise questions about privacy as well as validity. Even more generally, there may be distaste for tests as being too cold and impersonal or insulting for applicants for academic positions. Tests can also be difficult to locate or evaluate, and even more challenging to develop on your own.

These are complex issues that we address in more detail elsewhere (Rosse & Levin, 1997). In the current context we can summarize our perspective on employment testing as follows:

• Concerns about test fairness and privacy need to be taken seriously, but they need not be absolute obstacles to using tests of cognitive or noncognitive abilities. The key is to focus first on job-related requirements, and then to choose measures that have documented evidence of validity and test fairness. In some cases you may conclude that tests are the most reliable, valid, fair, and practical way to measure critical attributes.

• For the most part, concerns about test fairness and privacy do not apply to job knowledge tests or to performance tests (which we describe here as "work samples"). Job applicants in most employment settings also readily accept these types of tests.

• Useful approaches to assessing critical attributes should not be rejected simply because they're not typical in the academic world. Consider, as one example, the use of personality inventories, by which we mean the use of carefully developed, thoroughly validated, job-related inventories of personality attributes developed for employment rather than clinical purposes. Personality inventories are rarely used in higher education, even for attributes for which validities and reliabilities are higher than tools such as interviews. Does this mean that personality is less relevant to our jobs than to jobs in the nonacademic sector, where use of such inventories has become much more common in recent years? We find that unlikely, particularly for senior administrators, whose jobs seem to have much in common with the management positions for which personality inventories have been a mainstay. If a job involves attributes for which valid selection tests have been developed, it's worth strongly considering their use, whether or not these tests are common in academic settings.

REFERENCE AND BACKGROUND CHECKS FOR FINALIST REVIEW

Reference and background checks may occur both earlier and later in the hiring process. For example, you may want to talk with references before deciding whom to place on a short list of candidates, or it may be that your first contact with a candidate is through someone who recommends the person. Or you may decide that it's more efficient to check references only for the final list of candidates who have passed prior scrutiny. In many cases, it's both: you use initial checks as a screening device to eliminate those who lack fundamental requirements, and then go back a second time to verify credentials, follow up on questions that arise during interviews or campus visits, and deal with concerns about any potential Risk Factors. Regardless of when during the hiring process reference checking is done, the purpose is either to gather additional information that you can't get directly from the applicant or to verify information that he or she has provided.

Although it is convenient to obtain information directly from applicants—whether through application materials, interviews, or tests—there is some information that we should not expect an applicant to be able or willing to provide. For example, instructors (especially new ones) may honestly not have a good sense of how effective they are in the classroom. Asking colleagues or others who have observed the applicant's teaching is likely to be a more effective approach. Likewise, it may be useful to ask a former supervisor to provide perspective on a candidate's interpersonal skills, since we all have somewhat distorted views of our own social performance.

References can also be useful sources of information regarding qualifications that we cannot expect applicants to divulge, even if they are self-aware. For example, it's inconceivable that a candidate for a department manager position would list on his résumé that he'd been convicted of sexual harassment, and it's nearly as unlikely that he would volunteer this information during an interview. The only way to get this kind of information is to check with others who are in a position to know about and disclose it.

Verification of Critical Information

The example of prior sexual harassment raises a larger issue. In such an instance, the applicant "passively" misrepresents himself by failing to disclose relevant information, but the fault would be yours for failing to ask. In other cases applicants may either fail to provide requested information (for example, if you had asked in the application materials about prior convictions) or may claim to possess qualifications that they don't actually have.

One of the limitations of application blanks, vitae, and cover letters is that applicants are free to say whatever they think will make them look most attractive to you. Studies show that the resulting misrepresentation is rampant, with 20 to 25 percent of applicants making at least one major fabrication (LoPresto, Micham, & Ripley, 1986). Particularly common areas for misrepresentation include educational credentials, past salaries or job titles, and reasons for leaving prior jobs (Gatewood & Feild, 2000; Heneman, Heneman, & Judge, 1997). Misrepresentation is most likely on information that applicants assume you can't or won't verify and that is likely to have a bearing on their chances of getting the job or the munificence of your offer. For example, applicants are less likely to misrepresent the dates of prior employment than their reasons for leaving or the salaries they received on past jobs.

Some of the information that is likely to be misrepresented may not be very important; for example, prior salaries shouldn't be the basis for making hiring decisions and are thus irrelevant for most situations. Moreover, there is always the risk when conducting background information checks that you will be told information that is irrelevant, or even illegal to consider. Relying on your Performance Attributes Matrix to remind you what information you need to collect and then developing a structured Reference-Checking Form (such as that shown in Exhibit 5.5) can help keep both you and the reference provider focused on relevant information.

Exhibit 5.5. Example of Reference-Checking Form.

Applicant Name _____

Reference check by_____ Date: _____

Company Name_____

Contact Name_____ Phone: _____

Attributes	Response Ratings (Check one per attribute)			
	Good	Indifferent	Poor/ Problem	Wouldn't answer
Skill in oral communication Comments:				
Empathetic listening Comments:				
Ability to independently resolve unstructured problems Comments:				
Honesty and integrity Comments:				
Safety Orientation Comments:				

Dates of employment verified: Yes___   No___

Position verified: Yes___   No___

Reason for leaving verified: Yes___   No___

Source: Adapted from Rosse & Levin (1997).

Overcoming Obstacles to
Obtaining Background Information

Many people acknowledge the potential value of information provided by third parties but don't check references because they feel it will be impossible to get valid information from reference providers. Indeed, many employers, fearful of being sued for defamation of character if they say anything negative about prior employees, have instituted policies that they will report only the most basic information about former employees. Although verifying that candidates actually worked at a particular former employer may be useful, it is probably far less useful than information about the their performance and demeanor during that period.

Research and experience suggest that there are ways to break through this kind of resistance. One strategy is to make it very clear that the questions you are asking are job-relevant and asked in a way that the information provider can provide a clear and job-related answer. For example, asking if Sam is the "right kind of employee" makes it hard for the reference provider to know what information you're looking for. The provider may not know what kind of employee is "right" for your job, and may even suspect that you're using a subterfuge to get discriminatory information. In contrast, explaining the requirements for the job and then asking for specific examples of past behavior that the reference provider has observed, similar to Behavior Description Interview questions, can reassure the provider that the information being asked for is appropriate. This approach also makes it more likely that you'll get specific, nondiscriminatory information that you can use.

It is also prudent not to rely exclusively on the list of references provided by the candidate. Asking these individuals to provide the names of others who can provide useful comments—or contacting those that you and other search committee members may know at the candidate's prior place of employment—may produce more frank information about the candidate.

Another way to gather accurate information is to talk with sources who already know and trust you, and who are more willing to speak frankly about a candidate. When that's not possible, you can structure your request for information in a way that begins to build a relationship between you and the provider. Reminding the other person of the importance of making a good hire, the consequences of hiring the wrong person, and the fact that he or she has been in the same situation of needing to hire the right person for a job can create a greater willingness to provide you with relevant information. You might also reassure the reference provider that good information is in the interests of the applicant; no one gains from hiring employees who turn out to be unhappy or unproductive in their new job. Asking about an applicant's *relative* strengths and weaknesses on job-related attributes can help in this regard, since we all recognize that people are better at some tasks than at others.

When trying to develop a personal bond fails, you may be able to gently remind the reference provider that you have a legal obligation to uncover relevant information and that he or she has a corresponding obligation to disclose such information. Your obligation relates to a legal doctrine known as *negligent hiring,* which means that if you knew or should have been able to predict that an employee would later create problems for students, coworkers, or customers, you can be held partially responsible for that employee's actions. (A similar doctrine of *negligent retention* applies if you learn of this information after the person is hired and fail to take appropriate actions.) An example might be hiring a custodian who turns out to have a criminal record involving assault who then uses his access to students' rooms or restrooms to attack students. If you failed to check into his background (or worse, received hints about his past behavior and didn't follow up on them), you might be considered to have been negligent in your duties and partially responsible for the harm caused to others. A complementary responsibility applies to the person providing a reference. Providing a positive recommendation that fails to disclose risks that an individual presents may constitute *negligent recommendation,* meaning that the reference provider can be held partially accountable for the employee's subsequent misbehavior.

We don't want to overemphasize these legal considerations, important though they may be. The point is simply that you have a responsibility— to your institution, your employees and students, and legal authorities— to make a diligent effort to check out new employees, in terms of both performance qualifications and Risk Factors. You may not always be able to get all the information you want, but you need to exercise due diligence in attempting to gather this information.

SUMMARY

In this chapter we have reviewed how to use application materials, interviews, work samples, tests, and reference checks to evaluate applicants' qualifications. In doing so, our discussion has revolved around the two key themes of comprehensiveness and job-relatedness.

An effective hiring process uses a comprehensive set of selection tools. Most jobs, and particularly many of those in higher education, require a diverse set of qualifications for effective performance, and the comprehensiveness of the hiring system needs to be commensurate. No single hiring procedure can address all the attributes identified in most performance foundations, so the first step described in this chapter is to create a *Performance Attributes Matrix* that allows you to effectively match performance attributes with appropriate assessment procedures. This Performance Attributes Matrix also forms the basis for the hiring decision guide to be described in the next chapter.

The second critical step is to identify or develop valid hiring tools to assess the key attributes. Performance-based hiring tools are first of all clearly job-related, meaning that they have a demonstrable relationship to the critical job dimensions and attributes you identified in your performance foundation. This principle underlies the recommended practices for evaluating employment applications and vitae, developing interview questions and work samples, and even choosing or developing employment tests. Additional criteria for choosing among these hiring tools involve considerations of practicality (cost and time), perceived fairness, and potential adverse impact.

In this chapter you learned how to develop and collect a set of valid, job-related information on which fair and performance-based decisions can be made about whom to hire. It is to the process of using this information to make these decisions that we now turn.

A Practical Guide to Making Hiring Decisions

IF YOU'VE followed all the steps in the preceding chapters, you should now be looking at a relatively small set of finalists. Ironically, it is at this point—when it seems most of the hard work has been done—that many hiring problems occur. In this chapter we offer some guidelines to help you avoid the pitfalls that lurk in sight of the finish line and reach a successful conclusion to your recruiting efforts.

DECISION PITFALLS

There are three main reasons that hiring can go awry at the point of making a decision among top candidates. These three hazards are

- Hiring the best candidate in a substandard pool
- Abandoning the hiring criteria at the moment of decision
- Making ritual hiring decisions

In the following pages we consider each hazard, along with some potential solutions.

Hiring the Best Candidate in a Substandard Pool

This hazard arises from fooling oneself into thinking that the best of the candidates who end up on a short list will automatically be "good enough." This is easy to do when you've spent a lot of time and effort recruiting applicants, you're tired, and you needed someone in the position last week. This effect is compounded by the natural tendency to compare candidates to one another rather than to the standard of performance you established as part of your performance foundation.

These issues can become even more subtle when the process calls for candidates to be "ranked" relative to one another rather than "rated" against a standard. In *ranking,* the emphasis is on whether a candidate is first, second, or third when compared with other candidates and without regard for either an absolute standard or the magnitude of the differences between candidates. When *rating,* each candidate's attributes are evaluated against a standard of performance or qualifications. Always remember that, depending on the quality of your finalist pool, the highest ranked applicant may not be good enough.

Abandoning Your Hiring Criteria

Let's say that you're hiring an administrative assistant, and you've determined that the critical performance attributes include proficiency in word processing and spreadsheet programs, abilities in filing and record keeping, and sufficient interpersonal skills to interact effectively with faculty, students, and other staff. The position does not demand educational background beyond a baccalaureate degree. Your university is in a desirable location, so you get lots of applications, including one from an individual with a Ph.D. in comparative languages who can't get a job in his discipline and is waiting for his wife to complete her advanced degree. It might be tempting to hire him—perhaps imagining how you could put his skills to use in other areas of your department—without asking whether he would be a satisfied and satisfactory administrative assistant. If he doesn't have the requisite skills for the job, it makes little sense to hire him, regardless of the other "opportunities" he may seem to bring by virtue of his Ph.D.

Hiring criteria can also be tossed aside in the midst of battles about resource allocation. Being authorized to hire a department chair, for example, can be a tempting way to hire another theoretical physicist, but hiring a great physicist with no interest in acting as a chair is not likely to meet the needs of the department. If there are situations in which a position opening could provide multiple pathways to organizational excellence, these should be spelled out and decided on in advance. Thus, you could have a situation in which a classics department would benefit equally from a highly qualified senior person in either Latin or Greek. You could just as easily have a situation in which a Spanish and Portuguese department is losing one of only two Portuguese specialists, and hiring an excellent Spanish scholar just won't do.

Of course, these are some of the least damaging ways of changing your hiring criteria during the hiring process. Other common versions are to be blinded by a candidate's glib style (particularly if that's not relevant to the job), be put off by one candidate's race, gender, or political beliefs, or succumb to other biases.

As important as it is to make hiring decisions based on a careful analysis of performance qualifications, there may be situations in which you need to thoughtfully update or revise your initial performance foundation. Despite your best efforts to describe all the critical hiring attributes at the beginning of the process, you may become aware of other important attributes as the process continues, perhaps because their presence or absence in one candidate made their importance more obvious. The key in such a situation is to critically evaluate whether the new attribute is really critical or is essentially an excuse to hire a particular candidate. Going back to the performance foundation you created in Chapter Two—and getting reactions from others who are knowledgeable about the position—is the best way to make sure you're not fooling yourself. If you do add a new attribute to your list, be sure to go back and use it to fairly evaluate *all* of your finalist candidates.

Making Ritual Hiring Decisions

If you're overwhelmed by the information you've collected you may resort to a ritual approach to making hiring decisions. We've personally experienced more than one situation in which decision makers have a wealth of information on which to evaluate candidates and then resort to an oversimplified reliance on one or two data points. Decades of research by judgment and decision-making scholars demonstrates that humans are inherently weak when it comes to combining information to make a decision or diagnosis (Kleinmutz, 1990). Regardless of whether the decision makers are psychiatrists, physicians, mechanics, managers, or detectives, trying to combine information into a "clinical" (or judgmental) decision inevitably invites errors. Instead, using an *algorithm,* even a relatively crude one based on subjective judgments of how to combine the information, results in decisions that are both more consistent and more accurate.

In the remainder of this chapter we describe two decision models that allow you to create useful algorithms for deciding among applicants, one "categorical" in nature and one that is numerical. Both models are intended to simplify hiring decisions by establishing three prioritized criteria:

1. Screen out applicants who will create serious performance problems. Eliminating the clearly incompetent—as well as those with other performance problems—from your applicant pool can have a huge effect on performance. It also removes much of the uncertainty from your hiring, because it means that anyone who is left in the pool will be at least an acceptable hire.

2. Verify that the candidates who remain will at least satisfy your minimum requirements for work performance. Of course, that should be the case if you have eliminated those who are clearly unacceptable. Nevertheless, before offering any candidate a job, you want to double-check three critical and independent factors. The first is to make sure that you accurately set the level of acceptable performance. The second is to be sure you used accurate and valid methods to assess predicted performance. The third is to ensure that the information provided by candidates is accurate. Our research and research of others on faking in employment con-

texts indicate that it is prudent to proceed on the basis that a substantial proportion of any pool of candidates who appear to be qualified have in fact distorted one aspect or another of that appearance of competence (Levin & Zickar, 2002; Rosse, Stecher, Miller, & Levin, 1998). Identifying the individuals who are verifiably qualified at a sufficient level is generally easier than identifying the "best" applicants and in some situations may prove to be more cost-effective than hiring the "cream of the crop."

3. Once you are certain that you have a pool of qualified applicants, and if the quality of the pool provides you this luxury, you can then identify candidates who possess exceptional levels of critical qualifications that might make them preferred candidates to hire.

Most informal approaches to making hiring decisions begin with the third priority and never cover the first and second priorities. To make consistently effective hiring decisions, you must include all three priorities in their priority order. Omitting or delaying the first priority leads to hiring disasters, and doing the same for the second priority creates self-imposed hiring crises when suitable candidates are available. The hiring decision guide that follows will help you include all three priorities in every hire you make.

A HIRING DECISION GUIDE

Developing a systematic approach to decision making begins with the performance attributes matrix you developed for the job. The Performance Attributes Matrix guides you in using your judgment to evaluate the broad range and complexity of candidates' attributes in a systematic way, rather than confound all this complexity and reduce it to a single non-performance-based attribute we might call "gut feel."

The Performance Attributes Matrix also helps avoid the common mistake of confusing the performance *attributes* with the *assessment tools* used to measure them. Rather than saying that an applicant "did poorly" in an interview, you want to rate the person's performance on the particular *attributes* the interview was intended to assess. For example, your hiring decision might be based on scores for conscientiousness, work-specific knowledge, attention to detail, numerical reasoning, and computer operating skill. Some of these attributes may have been assessed by more than one hiring tool; for instance, work-specific knowledge may have been measured in both an interview and a work sample. Likewise, an interview might be designed to assess both conscientiousness and attention to detail; it's easy to imagine a candidate who excels on one of these traits but not on the other, a distinction that you don't want lost by assigning an "overall" interview rating.

In order to develop scores that are focused on attributes rather than tools, you can use the information from the Performance Attributes Matrix to develop composite scores for each of the attributes based on information you gained from the interview, vita, work sample, and so forth. The first step in doing so is developing a process for scoring each attribute.

Scoring Qualifications

As you evaluate each candidate on each attribute, a score or rating makes it easier to summarize and record judgments. Without recording scores, it's far easier to make decision-making errors that result from forgetting your evaluation, biasing your evaluation of one candidate against another, or aggregating your ratings into a single judgment to make it easier to remember. Imagine trying to remember your judgments of ten candidates on seven criteria without using some sort of scoring system!

Although most of us think of percentages or one-to-five rating scales when we think of scoring, we recommend you use three simple categories for evaluating most qualifications: *unacceptable,* minimally *acceptable,* and *desirable.*

- *Unacceptable.* Unacceptable means exactly what it sounds like: a candidate either lacks the minimum acceptable level of a critical attribute or is above a threshold on a relevant Risk Factor. The implication of an unacceptable rating on a critical attribute should be equally clear: *Don't hire candidates with unacceptable levels of any critical qualifications.*

Our experience has been that this simple rule is perhaps the most difficult for people to adopt initially but also the decision-making rule they find to be most powerful once they give it a good try. The rule is straightforward: once an applicant has a single unacceptable rating on a critical attribute (although not necessarily a single indicator of that attribute), he or she is out of the running. People often object, asking whether a candidate can't make up for unacceptable levels of one attribute by being particularly good in another area. This kind of compensatory effect may be appropriate if a person has at least minimal qualifications on each attribute but should never be allowed to operate when a person is truly unqualified on a particular attribute. If you're hiring a comptroller, no level of skill in making presentations can make up for ineptitude in accounting skills, nor will a wonderful research record compensate for a professor who misappropriates research funds. Unqualified means disqualified, and it's important to have a rating scale and a decision-making process that makes this explicit.

• *Acceptable.* Acceptable qualifications are those that will accomplish the most critical work outcomes, as defined in your performance foundation. When defining levels of qualifications, acceptable should not have a pejorative connotation. Acceptable ratings should reflect the level of qualifications shown by most incumbent employees (assuming you have a reasonably good performance management process), and it implies full capability to perform the job competently. Acceptable most emphatically does not imply hiring someone whose marginal performance impairs the ability of your program area to perform its work. This point is also important when considering legal requirements. No law requires that you hire someone who isn't qualified to do the job. But you are required to define that minimal level in fair, job-related (and therefore performance-related) terms. So you need to exercise care in defining acceptable ratings in terms that are neither too demanding nor too lax.

• *Desirable.* Your next step is to define the standards for what constitutes an outstanding performer, what we refer to as desirable levels of qualifications. As management expert Peter Drucker has pointed out, in order to hire excellent performers, you need to be clear in your mind first what excellent performance will look like (Drucker, 1967). By excellent performance we mean performance that has a disproportionate impact on the work of your organization; by definition, only a small number of applicants (or employees) will meet this standard.

More numerically oriented readers may worry that our unacceptable-acceptable-desirable rating system is too simple to adequately capture differences among applicants. In reality, it's about as precise an evaluation as you can make in most hiring decisions, given the inherent margin of error in assessment procedures. If you've done a good job developing a valid hiring system, a candidate with acceptable scores on all attributes will almost certainly perform better than a candidate with unacceptable ratings. At the same time, if you have two candidates who rate acceptably on most attributes and who both rate desirably on the same attribute, chances are that there won't be significant differences between them in job performance.

Creating Composite Attribute Ratings

Once you've scored each attribute measured by each hiring tool, the next step is to combine these ratings into composite ratings for each attribute. This may involve combining scores from different assessment tools that measure the same attribute. For example, you might have used a clerical test, an interview, and reference checks to assess attention to detail; now you want to combine the ratings from each of these assessments into a composite, or overall, rating of attention to detail for each candidate. In other cases it may involve combining scores from different assessors by, for example, combining the scores of six search committee members who all evaluated a candidate's leadership skills in a work sample.

One possible approach is to compute an arithmetic average of the scores from different tools or assessors. However, different tools may have different scoring systems, making an "average" score meaningless. For example, *dependability* scores might range from one to five on your structured interview, from one to four on your scored reference checking form, and from zero to a hundred on a personality inventory. How can you combine such disparate scoring systems to come up with an overall evaluation of applicants' dependability? An even more serious problem was noted earlier: arithmetic averaging allows unacceptable ratings to be compensated for (or worse, hidden) by high ratings.

We suggest an alternative approach that relies more on structured judgment and less on mathematical operations. The essence of this approach is to first assign ratings of *unacceptable, acceptable,* or *desirable* for each attribute on each assessment procedure, for each candidate. Then review all the ratings (across procedures) for each attribute and assign a composite *unacceptable-acceptable-desirable* rating for that attribute; repeat this procedure for each candidate. (Readers who would prefer a more numerically oriented system for combining scores on different hiring tools will find such an approach described in our earlier book, *High-Impact Hiring.*)

When making judgments like these it's important to look at the variance of scores across different assessment tools (or raters). For example, suppose you had two candidates—Phil and Elizabeth—being evaluated by a six-member search committee, and the scores for leadership skill looked like those in Exhibit 6.1. Both candidates have an average rating of *acceptable* on this attribute, but it's quite clear that only two of the committee members (Interviewers 3 and 4) view the candidates similarly. Situations like this should always be discussed before proceeding. If the variance is due to different standards being applied, then misunderstandings can arise after the hire. When different information is being conveyed to individual interviewers it could reflect different questions being asked, or it could mean that the candidate is trying to improve his or her chances by telling different interviewers what they might want to hear.

The situation can be more difficult when the discrepancies occur across different assessment tools. Let's return to our example of measuring attention to detail for an administrative assistant position with an interview, clerical test, and reference check. What do you do if a particular candidate receives *desirable* ratings for this attribute on the test and in the interview, but you hear from a former employer that he was sloppy and careless in his work? Unacceptable *composite* ratings on a critical attribute should eliminate a candidate, but unacceptable ratings on a particular assessment need to be treated with more caution. Any one hiring tool is fallible, so it is unfair (and potentially illegal) to reject a candidate

Exhibit 6.1. Variance in Interview Ratings of Leadership Skill.

| | Candidate | |
	Phil	Elizabeth
Interviewer 1	Acceptable	Desirable
Interviewer 2	Acceptable	Desirable
Interviewer 3	Acceptable	Acceptable
Interviewer 4	Acceptable	Acceptable
Interviewer 5	Acceptable	Unacceptable
Interviewer 6	Acceptable	Unacceptable

too quickly based on any one score, particularly if that score conflicts with other assessments of the same attribute. When you find conflicts between different ratings for a single attribute, or find a single tool rating a candidate as unacceptable, treat that as a sign to examine the situation in more depth.

When reconciling conflicting scores you need to consider both the pattern of scores and the validity of each source. You also need to ask yourself whether you need additional information. In the example of the search committee, you might ask yourself whether Interviewers 5 and 6 have any biases against Elizabeth, and you might also have the committee share the information they have and see whether a second round of scores reaches more agreement. In the example of the reference provider, you might ask yourself whether, on the one hand, the reference provider might have a bias with regard to the candidate or, on the other hand, the candidate *knows* how to work with good attention to detail but didn't work in that way in the last job. In turn, this could be because of problems specific to the last workplace, or could be a more general pattern. You would be wise to seek out some additional references, and even call the candidate back in for follow-up interviewing that targets this skill area.

Using Attribute Ratings to Make Hiring Decisions

Once you've developed a composite score for each applicant on each attribute, the next step is to combine this information in a way that will allow you to make a hiring decision. If you are fortunate enough to have candidates who score in the desirable range on every important attribute, they should be immediately and strongly considered for employment. Candidates who score desirably on some attributes and at least acceptably on all attributes should be put in a second group to be reviewed carefully, possibly as back-up candidates. Candidates with *acceptable* scores on all attributes but no desirable scores are considered last. Candidates who score unacceptably on any important attribute should already have been removed from further consideration, regardless of whether other attributes are rated as *acceptable* or desirable. This method is not only intuitive and straightforward to use but is also well established to provide good results under a variety of conditions (Cronbach & Gleser, 1965; Gatewood & Feild, 2000; Gigerenzer, Todd, & ABC Research Group, 1998).

You can also use variants of this basic approach, depending on how many people you need to hire, how many candidates are available at what level of predicted performance, and how much different levels of qualifications affect performance. If you need to hire more people than you have qualified applicants, your approach is straightforward: you simply hire all candidates who have at least *acceptable* ratings on each of the critical attributes. Then you either go back out and recruit more applicants, or consult your PATH for other alternatives.

When you have more qualified applicants than openings—the more typical situation when hiring faculty or administrators—the process becomes more complex. Creating a Hiring Decision Guide can make it easier for you to compare candidates' packages of skills against each other and with your needs.

Using a Hiring Decision Guide

A Hiring Decision Guide is a graphic representation of candidates' qualifications on the critical performance attributes for a job; an example is shown in Exhibit 6.2. A Hiring Decision Guide makes it easy to compare all of your finalists against your hiring standards, and also facilitates making decisions about which candidates should receive an offer and in what order. You can create a Hiring Decision Guide as follows:

• List the critical attributes across the top of the chart, creating one column for every attribute. If there are significant differences in importance between critical attributes, the most important attribute should be listed in the first column, second most important in the second column, and so on. Don't worry too much about this—if all the attributes are about equal in importance, they can go in any order on the chart.

• List the names of the applicants in the first column of the table so that there is a row for each applicant.

• Fill in the composite ratings for each applicant on each attribute. For most purposes the *desirable* and *acceptable* ratings should work fine. Applicants with any unacceptable ratings who have not already been removed from the pool should be eliminated when these ratings show up on the table.

If all of the critical attributes are about equally important, you can rank-order your candidates by simply counting the number of attributes on which they have desirable scores. For example, in Figure 6.2, Anne would be ranked as the first choice on the basis of four desirable ratings, Moesha would be ranked second with three desirable ratings, and Juan is third with one desirable rating. Note that Paul and Lynn each received an undesirable rating and are eliminated.

As you can see, this is a simple method that helps you differentiate among candidates and often provides you with enough detail to make final decisions. If not, three approaches can be used to make finer distinctions. One approach is to add to your decision table any desired (that is, relevant but noncritical) attributes that you identified in your performance foundation. For instance, you or your committee may have specified that a candidate for a deanship must have administrative experience, a prior record of academic achievement, proven ability to fundraise, and ability to resolve conflicts. As desirable, but not essential, attributes, you might have included attributes such as activity in current research or familiarity with public (or private) higher education. In most real-world settings, were you to be fortunate to locate two experienced administrators, each with a strong academic background and some experience at fundraising, you would probably be able to differentiate between them based on ability to resolve conflicts. If not, though, you could then move to your

Exhibit 6.2. Hiring Decision Guide.

			Critical Attributes			
Candidate	Oral Communication	Written Communication	Empathetic Listening	Problem Solving	Honesty, Integrity	Safety Orientation
Anne	Desirable	Desirable	Desirable	Desirable	Acceptable	Acceptable
Paul	Desirable	Desirable	Desirable	Unacceptable	Acceptable	Acceptable
Juan	Acceptable	Desirable	Acceptable	Acceptable	Acceptable	Acceptable
Moesha	Desirable	Acceptable	Desirable	Desirable	Acceptable	Acceptable
Lynn	Desirable	Acceptable	Desirable	Acceptable	Unacceptable	Acceptable

desired characteristics and see whether either was differentiable as an active researcher or as someone with familiarity with your kind of institution.

A second approach is to make decisions based on certain characteristics of a criterion, once acceptability has been reached. Once minimally acceptable competency is reached on all attributes, performance is often rooted in trade-offs, combinations, and blends of different attributes. If so, you want to find the combinations that provide a good fit with desired performance. For example, when hiring a faculty member you probably want minimally acceptable performance in the traditional core areas of research, teaching, and service. Once those criteria are met, your choice among candidates may hinge on the relative weight given in your unit to research or to the match of different candidates' research areas with those of others in the department. Applicants can be evaluated on these attributes in the same way you evaluated them on the critical attributes.

A third tie-breaker approach is to make finer distinctions among the critical attributes, assuming that you have rated some attributes as significantly more important than others and that you want to give more weight to these. To do so, modify your decision table as follows:

1. At the top of the table, note the most important attribute with a Roman numeral I, the second most important with a Roman numeral II, and so on. (Or, if you prefer, prepare a new table in which the most important attribute is listed in the first column, the second most important in the second column, and so on.) You can do so by using the importance ratings you developed in Chapter Two.

2. Count the number of attributes rated as desirable for each candidate. (You may want to tally these at the right side of the table.)

3. Circle or highlight the desirable level ratings for the most important attribute.

4. Consider first those candidates who have high numbers of desirable ratings and have attained desirable ratings on the most important attributes.

5. To make finer distinctions within this group, start with the candidate who has a desirable rating for the most critical attribute and the highest number of desirable level ratings. If you want even finer detail, of those who attained desirable ratings on the most important attribute and high overall numbers of desirable ratings, consider first those who had the highest ratings on the *second* most important attribute.

6. Once you've considered the first candidate, you can continue down through the rest of the candidates with desirable ratings on the most important attribute. Then you can proceed to those with desirable ratings on the second, third, fourth, and successive most important attributes. You can make finer ratings as needed using the methods above.

In practice, sophisticated weighted systems rarely outperform the kind of simple decision approaches described in Exhibit 6.2. People may use various skills in different ways to reach similar outcomes, and even the best hiring tools have substantial measurement error. A performance-oriented selection system can help you hire excellent candidates but is less able to distinguish which of two excellent candidates is better than the other.

AN IMPORTANT CAVEAT

This chapter, and this book, are predicated on the belief that any dean, department chair, administrator, or faculty member can make better hiring decisions by understanding and following the principles of performance orientation, systematic information gathering, and effective decision making. At the same time, we do not want to suggest that following these principles and guidelines will eliminate hiring mistakes. You can certainly anticipate that *fewer* hiring mistakes will occur, but expecting to eliminate such errors is not only unrealistic but counterproductive.

Hiring mistakes are inevitable due to inherent limitations in measuring and predicting human behavior. Not only is it difficult to assess applicants accurately but also different employees with diverse sets of qualifications may develop different routes to success by using strengths in one area to compensate for deficiencies in another. And of course people and jobs change, throwing all of this into a dynamic flux.

Under these circumstances, it is sometimes the case that a newly hired employee does not work out for reasons that could not have been anticipated with even the most systematic approach to hiring. We recall two faculty at different universities, each of whom had the best of training, strong publication records, and excellent teaching skills—yet both left the jobs for which they were hired. One person determined only after gaining a few years' experience at a major university that his interests and personality were better suited to a research laboratory than to a university. The other developed a serious illness that prevented her from continuing to work. Neither outcome could reasonably have been predicted from even the most rigorous applications of the principles described in this book.

Placing undue faith in any one hiring decision can also blind you to employees who are not being productive. The reality is that even the most accurate hiring procedures—those few with validity coefficients greater than 0.30 or 0.40—are still fallible at some level. You often can't be as selective as you'd like to be (because of tight labor markets, budget constraints, time pressures, and so forth), and many jobs for which you're hiring are simply not easy to perform even with post-hiring coaching and training. Put all these factors together and the performance yield— that is, the likelihood that a new hire will be successful—will generally be in the 70 to 85 percent range. That is, even if all appropriate hiring practices are followed, 15 to 30 percent of hires will not work out (Levin & Rosse, 2001; Taylor & Russell, 1939).

In the final chapter that follows, we offer guidelines for maximizing the likelihood that those you hire will succeed, while also accounting for the fact that a substantial number of hires will not be successful or will not remain in your institution as long as you had hoped. The last step in hiring always takes place *after* the hire.

Hanging On to Your Hires

YOU CAN have as much impact on the outcome of your hiring process by what you do *after* deciding who to hire as you did *before* the decision gets made. In this final chapter, we offer some pointers about wrapping up the hiring process, bringing your new hire on board, and beginning the development of a successful employment relationship.

WRAPPING UP THE HIRING PROCESS

As you evaluated your list of finalists, one of the questions in your mind might have been whether each finalist would actually accept the job if it was offered. If it wasn't in your mind then, it should be considered now, because it is frequently the case that the candidate you want to hire needs to be persuaded that your job is in his or her best interest.

Marketing the Job to Your Candidate

At this point in the hiring process there is often a subtle change in strategy. Your prior activities have been primarily focused on evaluation of the candidate, while doing so as part of a process that sought to create a positive (yet realistic) impression. Now your emphasis needs to shift away from evaluation, which has been completed, to influence.

You have already identified what is likely to make your institution and this job attractive to the applicants you want to hire. You can now add to this analysis what you know about your preferred candidate to determine how best to market the job specifically to him or her. You might have learned, for example, that providing particular laboratory facilities is especially important to a star researcher you're trying to attract, that your first choice for an administrative staff position wants a delayed starting date in order to complete initiatives in his current institution, or that a faculty candidate really wants to teach certain courses in her first two years. Identifying preferences such as these may be critical for convincing your candidate to take the job, and may be easier to provide than other inducements over which you have less control (such as salary, benefits, or your geographical location).

As academics we may not like to think of our institutions as commodities to be sold like toothpaste, and certainly care must be taken not to create such an impression. Nonetheless, it's important to remember that "selling" the job can sometimes make the difference between the candidate taking the position you are offering rather than one at a competing institution. Even if the candidate is already inclined to take the job, the extra attention is flattering and likely to increase excitement about the opportunity.

Communicating Your Decision

Once you've decided whom you want, it's important to convey that decision to the candidate as quickly as possible, particularly if the candidate is likely to be receiving offers from other schools. This should be done first in a telephone call, usually made by the search committee chair or the immediate supervisor.

Not only does a phone call provide the quickest communication, but it also allows you to get an immediate sense of the candidate's interest. If candidates indicate that they've taken another job, you can thank them for their interest and immediately move on to a backup candidate if one exists. If a candidate indicates some reservations, this provides you with an opportunity to do some persuading. You may be able to modify your offer to meet desires of which you were not aware, something that is much more difficult to do once a formal offer letter has been approved and sent.

In your call you should also discuss a mutually agreeable deadline for deciding on your offer. The deadline should allow enough time for the candidate to evaluate your offer and consult with family or others affected, but short enough to allow you to pursue a backup candidate if your first choice declines. Although it may be tempting to demand a quick decision to avoid competing with other offers the candidate may subsequently receive, this strategy can backfire if the candidate feels pressured and decides to decline your offer and wait.

A formal offer letter that describes the conditions of employment in detail should follow the phone conversation as soon as possible. Since this is a legally binding document, it is wise to use a template that has been reviewed by legal counsel. It's a good idea to follow up the letter with a phone call to answer any questions or objections the candidate may have.

It's also important to communicate with the applicants you've decided not to hire. Anyone who is clearly unqualified should be sent a polite "thank you" letter as soon as possible. However, if you identified a set of acceptable finalists, it's wise to postpone contacting them until your first choice returns a signed letter of acceptance.

Handling Rejection: What If Your First Choice Turns You Down?

Your hiring decision guide is a useful tool to have when making job offers, because it allows you to keep track of qualified backup candidates, as well as an order in which to make backup offers. Moreover, the guide will keep you from making backup offers to candidates who are unacceptable to begin with. If you find that you have no acceptable backup candidates, you need to reopen a search, and make whatever temporary staffing adjustments are necessary in the interim, rather than offering the job to a candidate who is unacceptable.

BRINGING THE NEW HIRE ON BOARD

Recruiting a new organizational member is a lot of work, so there's a natural tendency to sigh with relief and move on to other priorities when your candidate accepts your offer. Although the hardest work is over, there are still things you can do to increase the likelihood that the new hire will be successful.

People quickly form a first impression of the job that can be hard to change. The first weeks after accepting or starting a job are also the times that they are most subject to "buyer's remorse," as they ruminate about whether they made the right choice in coming to work at your institution. Private-sector companies have thought about how to best welcome new staff members into a work group. We're not suggesting that all private-sector firms do it right, but here's a list of ten tips, many of which are commonly used in the private sector, that can help you get started with new hires in ways that increase the likelihood of successful outcomes:

1. Help new hires prepare by sending them information about your institution and community, particularly if they will be relocating. Information about housing, schools, and spousal employment opportunities are common issues that new employees have to address. The more you can help your new hires with these issues, the quicker they can become productive.

2. Make sure new hires have a functioning workspace before the first day of work. If they come for the job of a lifetime and are instead left wandering the halls, unable to use the telephone or log onto a computer, and are sent traipsing around the campus through the rain to pick up keys, it's not the beginning they were hoping for.

3. Be there to meet and greet new hires on their first day. You may be immediately "turning them over" to someone else, but your meeting them lets both the new hires and the people they are connecting with for the first time know that the new hires belong, and that you care about things getting taken care of. If they will be working with others on their first day, let the new hires know that you will stop back—at the end of the first morning, or the first day, or the next morning. In addition to helping with any problems or questions, it's often a nice gesture to take the person to lunch or to some other informal social event.

4. Help new hires get oriented to your organization. This includes everything from getting a better sense of the mission of the insti-

tution to figuring out where to get supplies. Unlike in private sector firms, formal orientation programs are rare in higher education, despite the reality that most colleges and universities are large, complex, and even intimidating organizations. Don't assume that candidates who have spent much of their life in higher education will automatically be able to figure out the idiosyncrasies of *your* institution. If your college or unit doesn't have some basic orientation materials, consider creating them yourself; the effort will certainly pay off over the years. At the least, ask yourself what you'd need to know if you were a new hire, and make sure to go over that information with each new hire.

5. Arrange for new hires to meet people over the first few weeks. This helps create a welcoming environment, and can also solve many orientation problems by giving new jobholders a sense of whom to go to with questions.

6. Provide, where appropriate, clear expectations of performance. Depending on the nature of the job, new hires may need either specific goal setting and instruction or more general guidance (for example, about teaching expectations at your institution, or about guidelines for tenure and promotion decisions).

7. Provide adequate training. In some cases, this may involve immediate and specific training in equipment or procedures. In other cases, it may be longer-term developmental opportunities such as teaching or research workshops. In either case, it's important to remember that opportunities for development are among the issues that are consistently related to employee retention (Gallup Organization, 1998).

8. Take some time to meet the new hire after the first day and during the first week or two for a cup of coffee or a meal. Along with giving them some social contact at the time when it may be scarcest for them, you are giving them an opportunity to talk with you informally about how things are going and to take care of little problems before they become bigger.

9. Provide some early evaluation, even if informal, during the first month to six weeks, first three months, six months, and year. Doing so is also appropriate for faculty and administration hires, even if it takes the form of taking the time to sit down and ask how things are going and then taking necessary actions.

10. Don't overreact to performance or personal issues during the first few weeks or months. A new job always presents challenges, and these are compounded if the job involves relocation, particularly if a whole family is affected. Even among experienced employees, the combination of the stress of a new job, often a new location, coupled with any insecurity or shyness can bring out people's rough spots just when they want to do their best. You'll need to give new hires a chance to settle in order to get a full picture of how they perform day-to-day.

Your efforts with new hires will not only help get them off on a good foot but will also help you get the significant people in their lives on your side from the outset. What are the questions that every new job-holder will be asked by family and friends during their first day, week, and month? How's the new job? Are they treating you well there? How are you getting on? Your efforts will help ensure that the answers they give to these questions are positive ones that reinforce with themselves and those around them that the decision to come to your institution was a good one.

MAINTAINING THE RELATIONSHIP

Our central theme in this book is that people—staff, faculty, and administrators—are critical to effectiveness in higher education. Hiring the right people is essential, but it's not the whole story. Retaining top performers and maintaining peak performance are also critical and complex enough to deserve its own treatment. In fact, we have provided an in-depth treatment of these issues in a separate volume: *Talent Flow: A Strategic Guide to Keeping Good Employees, Helping Them Grow, and Letting Them Go* (Levin and Rosse, 2001). We can briefly summarize some of the key points of *Talent Flow* as follows:

• Taking a careful, systematic approach to hiring is an essential step toward reducing unwanted turnover by increasing the likelihood of a good "match" among skills, interests, and opportunities. However, as you learned in the last chapter, even the best hiring system will result in some unfavorable outcomes, including both voluntary and involuntary turnover. Moreover, people will inevitably leave their jobs at some point, whether by moving to another job or through retirement.

• Turnover is not inherently undesirable, even from an employer's perspective, despite the costs it inevitably creates. Your goal is to minimize turnover among productive performers, while encouraging turnover among those who are not performing adequately or who are acting in a counterproductive manner.

• Causes of turnover can be categorized into Environment, Individual, and Workplace factors, each of which has different implications. *Environment* factors (such as a strong job market) are pervasive, powerful, and generally outside anyone's control, although you can reduce their impact by anticipating and planning for environmentally caused turnover. Research shows that *Individual* causes of turnover (such as communication style or work values) are less important than we commonly assume and often serve as a scapegoat to divert distraction from what managers and administrators can more readily affect: *Workplace* factors (such as rewarding work, supportive working relationships, and safe and comfortable working conditions).

• Work should be designed and managed so as to minimize sources of job dissatisfaction, and steps (such as satisfaction surveys) should be taken to detect and respond to emergent sources of dissatisfaction.

• Even with the best efforts at preventing morale problems, some dissatisfaction will inevitably occur. Your "second line of defense" is to encourage people to respond to this dissatisfaction in constructive rather than counterproductive ways. The most constructive approach— *Problem Solving*—involves proactive attempts to resolve the source of the dissatisfaction. Less constructive approaches include *Exit* (quitting or transferring); *Avoidance* (neglecting job responsibilities, chronic absenteeism or tardiness); *Capitulation* (giving up; becoming increasingly disengaged from work responsibilities); and *Retaliation* (against colleagues, students, or others).

- Whether individuals respond in constructive or counterproductive ways depends in large part on Workplace factors. Individuals who trust administrators and managers are more likely to attempt Problem-Solving solutions, whereas those who don't are more likely either to Exit (if they can find alternative jobs) or engage in Capitulation, Avoidance, or Retaliation (depending on their predispositions and on what the system tends to reward and punish).

The implications of these points are closely aligned with what you have learned throughout this book. Fundamental to successful job performance is having employees who are qualified, motivated, and satisfied. The hiring system you have learned in this book provides the foundation for this performance formula by helping you identify and select candidates with the right qualifications for effective performance and long-term satisfaction. The hires you make as an academic administrator are one of your most important legacies to your institution and to higher education. Taking a systematic approach to hiring for performance will help ensure that your own work is enhanced by colleagues who are productive and satisfied, and that you establish a legacy of hiring for high performance.

REFERENCES

Arvey, R. D., & Campion, J. E. (1982). The employment interview: A summary and review of recent literature. *Personnel Psychology, 35,* 281–322.

Carson, K. P., & Stewart, G. L. (1995). Job analysis and the sociotechnical approach to quality: A critical examination. *Journal of Quality Management, 1*(1), 49–64.

Chickering, A. W., & Gamson, Z. F. (1994). Seven principles for good practice in undergraduate education. In K. A. Feldman & M. B. Paulsen (Eds.), *Teaching and learning in the college classroom* (pp. 255–262). Needham Heights, MA: Ginn Press.

Cronbach, L. J., & Gleser, G. (1965). *Psychological testing and personnel decisions* (2nd ed.). Urbana, IL: University of Illinois Press.

Cropanzano, R., & Greenberg, J. (1997). Progress in organizational justice: Tunneling through the maze. In L. T. Robertson & C. L. Cooper (Eds.), *International review of industrial and organizational psychology* (pp. 317–372). New York: Wiley.

Drucker, P. F. (1967). *The effective executive.* New York: Harper-Collins.

Gallup Organization (1998). Employees speak out on job training: Findings of a new, nationwide survey. Lincoln, NE: The Gallup Organization.

Gatewood, R. D., & Feild, H. S. (2000). *Human resource selection* (5th ed.). Fort Worth: Dryden Press.

Gigerenzer, G., Todd, P. M., & ABC Research Group (Eds.). (1998). *Simple heuristics that make us smart.* New York: Oxford University Press.

Greenberg, J. (1987). A taxonomy of organizational justice theories. *Academy of Management Review, 12,* 9–22.

Guzzo, R. A., & Dickson, M. W. (1996). Teams in organizations: Recent research on performance and effectiveness. *Annual Review of Psychology, 47,* 307–338.

Harvey, R. J. (1991). Job analysis. In M. D. Dunnette & L. M. Hough (Eds.), *Handbook of industrial and organizational psychology* (2nd ed., Vol. 2). Palo Alto, CA: Consulting Psychologists Press.

Heneman, H. G., Heneman, R. L., & Judge, T. A. (1997). *Staffing organizations* (2nd ed.). Burr Ridge, IL: Irwin.

Highhouse, S., & Johnson, M. A. (1996). Gain/loss asymmetry and riskless choice: Loss aversion in choices among job finalists. *Organizational Behavior and Human Decision Processes, 68,* 225–233.

Hough, L. M. (1984). Development and validation of the "Accomplishment Record" method of selecting and promoting professionals. *Journal of Applied Psychology, 69,* 135–146.

Huffcutt, A. I., Weekley, J. A., Wiesner, W. H., DeGroot, T. G., & Jones, C. (2001). Comparison of situational and behavior description interview questions for higher-level positions. *Personnel Psychology, 54,* 619–644.

Hulin, C. L., Henry, R. A., & Noon, S. L. (1990). Adding a dimension: Time as a factor in the generalizability of predictive relationships. *Psychological Bulletin, 107*(3), 328–340.

Janz, T. (1986). *Behavioral description interviewing.* Boston: Allyn & Bacon.

Kaplin, W. A., & Lee, B. A. (1995). *The law of higher education.* San Francisco: Jossey-Bass.

Kaplowitz, R. A. (1986). *Selecting college and university personnel: The quest and the questions.* ASHE-ERIC Higher Education Report No. 8. Washington, D.C.: Association for the Study of Higher Education.

Kleinmutz, B. (1990). Why we still use our heads instead of our formulas: Towards an integrative approach. *Psychological Bulletin, 107,* 296–310.

Latham, G. P., Saari, L., Pursell, E., & Campion, M. (1980). The situational interview. *Journal of Applied Psychology, 65,* 422–427.

Leatherman, C. (2000). Part-timers continue to replace full-timers on college faculties. *Chronicle of Higher Education, 46*(21), A18–A19.

Levin, R. A., & Rosse, J. G. (2001). *Talent flow: A strategic approach to keeping good employees, helping them grow, and letting them go.* San Francisco: Jossey-Bass.

Levin, R. A., & Zickar, M. J. (2002). Investigating self-presentation, lies, and bullshit: Understanding faking and its effects on selection decisions using theory, field research, and simulation. In J. F. Brett & F. Drasgow (Eds.), *The psychology of work: Theoretically-based empirical research* (pp. 253–276). Mahwah, NJ: Erlbaum.

LoPresto, R., Micham, D. E., & Ripley, D. E. (1986). *Reference checking handbook.* Alexandria, VA: American Society for Personnel Administration.

Marchese, T. J., & Lawrence, J. F. (1988). *The search committee handbook: A guide to hiring administrators.* Washington, D.C.: American Association of Higher Education.

Marcus, D. L. (2001, March 19). Why a good college chief is hard to find: Schools look for presidents. And look again. *US News & World Report, 46.*

McDaniel, M. A., Whetzel, D. L., Schmidt, F. L., & Maurer, S. D. (1994). The validity of employment interviews: A comprehensive review and meta-analysis. *Journal of Applied Psychology, 79,* 599–616.

Miller, J. L. (1995). Organizational commitment of temporary workers: A combined identity theory and psychological contract perspective. Unpublished Dissertation, University of Colorado at Boulder, Boulder, CO.

Morgan, R. B., & Smith, J. E. (1996). *Staffing the new workplace.* Milwaukee, WI: ASQC Quality Press.

Murray, J. P. (1999). Interviewing to hire competent community college faculty. *Community College Review, 27*(1), 41–56.

Nelson, M. (1997). The real problem with tenure is incompetent faculty hiring. *Chronicle of Higher Education, 44*(12), B4–B5.

Rose, R. G. (1993). *Practical issues in employment testing.* Odessa, FL: Psychological Assessment Resources.

Rosse, J. G., & Hulin, C. L. (1985). Adaptation to work: An analysis of employee health, withdrawal and change. *Organizational Behavior and Human Decision Processes, 36*(4), 324–347.

Rosse, J. G., & Levin, R. A. (1997). *High-impact hiring: A comprehensive guide to performance-based hiring.* San Francisco: Jossey-Bass.

Rosse, J. G., Miller, J. L., & Stecher, M. D. (1994). A field study of job applicants' reactions to personality and cognitive ability testing. *Journal of Applied Psychology, 79,* 987–992.

Rosse, J. G., Stecher, M. D., Miller, J. L., & Levin, R. A. (1998). The impact of response distortion on pre-employment personality testing and hiring decisions. *Journal of Applied Psychology, 83,* 634–644.

Sanchez, J. I. (1994). From documentation to innovation: Reshaping job analysis to meet emerging business needs. *Human Resource Management Review, 4*(1), 51–74.

Schmidt, P. (1997). A federal appeals court upholds California measure barring racial preferences. *Chronicle of Higher Education, 43*(32), A28–A29.

Schmidt, P. (1998). California judge upholds law allowing 2-year colleges to use hiring preferences. *Chronicle of Higher Education, 45*(16), A52.

Schneider, A. (1999). Wisconsin loses case over race-based hiring. *Chronicle of Higher Education, 46*(4), A18.

Simon, H. A. (1976). *Administrative behavior: A study of decision-making processes in administrative organizations* (3rd ed.). New York: Free Press.

Sovereign, K. L. (1994). *Personnel law* (3rd ed.). Englewood Cliffs: Prentice Hall.

Springer, A. D. (2002). Update on affirmative action in higher education: A current legal overview. Available: http://www.aaup.org/Issues/Affirmative Action/aalegal.htm.

Taylor, H. C., & Russell, J. T. (1939). The relationship of validity coefficients to the practical effectiveness of tests in selection. *Journal of Applied Psychology, 23,* 565–578.

Van der Vorm, P. T. (2001). The well-tempered search: Hiring faculty and administrators for mission. *Academe, 87*(3), 34–36.

Waggaman, J. S. (1983). Faculty recruitment, retention, and fair employment: Obligations and opportunities. ASHE-ERIC Higher Education Research Report No. 2. Washington, DC: Association for the Study of Higher Education.

Wanous, J. P. (1980). *Organizational entry: recruitment, selection and socialization of newcomers.* Reading, MA: Addison-Wesley.

Wilson, R. (1999). How a university created 95 faculty slots and scaled back its use of part-timers. *Chronicle of Higher Education, 46*(9), A18–A20.

Wolverton, M., Gmelch, W. H., & Montez, J. (2001). The changing nature of the academic deanship. *ASHE-ERIC Higher Education Reports, 28*(1), 1–144.

INDEX

A

ABC Research Group, 127
Abilities, 29–30
Adarand Constructors, Inc. v. Pena, 80
Advertising: classified, 50–51; costs and effectiveness of, 51–52
Affirmative action, 78–80
After the hire, 133–140; communicating decisions, 134–135; helping new hires into organization, 135–139; marketing job to candidates, 133–134; retaining staff and faculty, 138–140; when your first choice declines, 135
Age, 67, 99
Age Discrimination in Employment Act, 67
Americans with Disabilities Act (ADA): accommodating disabilities with, 72–73; provisions of, 68
Applicants, 20–32, 85–115; analyzing ability to meet job outcomes, 22–23; approaches for attracting, 50–51; availability when hiring, 57; becoming employer of choice for, 48–49; certainty- and uncertainty-based hiring of, 23–25; effective hiring and adequate numbers of, 37; employment testing of, 107–109; Fit Factors for potential, 22, 26–

28; helping success of new, 135–138; hiring best from substandard pool, 118; hiring tools and privacy of, 92; identifying attributes needed in, 28–31, 85–87; in-depth evaluation of, 96–109; initial screening of, 93–96; linking hiring to mission, 21–22; marketing job to chosen, 133–134; misrepresenting critical information, 111; realistic job previews for, 49–50; reference and background checks for finalists, 110–115; reference-checking form for, 112; Risk Factors of, 22, 25–26; scoring qualifications for job, 122–124; screening unqualified, 120–121; search chair and consideration of, 19; tailoring benefits to attract, 35–36; work samples, 105–107; writing job descriptions for, 32; wrong reasons for hiring, 20–21. *See also* Attracting talent; Performance Attributes Matrix
Application forms, 87, 94, 95–96
Arvey, R. D., 97
Attracting talent, 37–60; breaking cycle of crisis hiring, 38–48; building recruiting foundation, 48–50; creating adequate applicant pool, 58, 59; developing recruiting

Attracting talent (*continued*)
strategies, 50–56, 59; encouraging
diverse workforce, 56–59; overview,
37–38. *See also* Diversity; Recruiting

B

Background checks, 110–115; over-
coming obstacles to, 113–115;
reference-checking form, 112; talking with references, 110, 113–115;
verifying critical information,
111–112
Bakke case, 78–79
Behavior Description Interviewing, 98,
101
Benefits as compensation, 35–36
Biases in interviews, 97–98
Budgeting interview time, 103

C

Campion, J. E., 97
Campion, M., 101
Carson, K. P., 23
Certainty-based hiring, 23–25
Chair of search committees: determining role of committee, 14–15; role
of, 15–16, 18–19. *See also* Search
committees
Challenges in hiring, 3–10; avoiding
warm-body hiring, 8–9; in business
schools, 40–41; certainty- and
uncertainty-based hiring, 23–25;
decision making and, 7–8; ineffectiveness of ritual hiring, 9–10; legal
perspectives, 66–67; moral-ethical
perspectives, 65–66; performance
orientation and, 5–7; in private
industry vs. higher education, 4;
systematic information gathering
and, 7. *See also* Legal issues
Chickering, A. W., 23
Civil Rights Act (Title VII), 68
Cognitive skills evaluation, 8
Common law, 67, 69
Common law of agency, 69
Communications: announcing hiring

decisions, 136–137; informing
applicants of search process, 96
Compensation, 32–36; about, 32;
benefits as part of total, 35–36;
equity considerations, 33–34; listing in recruiting ads, 52
Composition of search committees,
15–16
Constitutional law, 67
Continuous hiring, 45–46
Contract law, 69
Coordinating with other interviewers,
104–105
Costs: of hiring by search committee,
14; of recruiting ads, 51–52
Cover letters, 94
Credit history, 99–100
Criminal records, 99
Crisis hiring, 38–48; anticipating hir-
ing needs vs., 39–41; developing
alternative strategies for, 42; fighting
fire analogy for, 38–39; replace-
ment planning as alternative, 42–
43; unanticipated hiring needs and
PATH, 41–48, 59
Cronbach, L. J., 127
Cropanzano, R., 33

D

Decision making, 117–133; abandoning hiring criteria during, 118–119;
agreement on outcomes of job
search, 17–18; creating composite
attribute ratings, 124–126; determining search committee's role,
14–15; evaluating duties of job,
23, 36; hazards of, 117; hiring best
from substandard pool, 118; Hiring
Decision Guide for, 127–131; hiring from attribute ratings, 126–
127; making good choices, 7–8;
managing search committees', 17;
scoring applicant qualifications,
122–124; screening out unqualified
applicants, 120–121; when your
first choice declines, 135

Defendants, 73

Defending hiring practices, 74–78; in disparate impact cases, 75, 76, 77; in disparate treatment cases, 75

DeGroot, T. G., 102

Desirable qualifications, 123–124

Developing PATH, 42

Dickson, M. W., 17

Disabilities: accommodating, 72–73; Americans with Disabilities Act, 68; preemployment questions about, 100

Discrimination, 70–72; defined, 70–72; disparate impact, 72; disparate treatment, 71–72; filing complaints, 73–78

Disparate impact: about, 72; defending against charges of, 75, 76, 77; evaluating hiring procedures for, 81; Four-fifths Rule and, 76; plaintiff's burden of proof in, 74

Disparate treatment: defending against charges of, 75; examples of, 71–72; plaintiff's burden of proof in, 74

Diversity, 56–59; few people available when hiring, 57; slow talent flows and, 56–57

Documenting hiring procedures, 81

Drucker, Peter, 123–124

Dysfunctional approaches to hiring, 20–21

E

EEO laws and prohibited practices, 69–73; listing of major laws, 68; protected characteristics, 69–70

Employees: applicant referrals by, 54–55; equity in compensation for, 34; faculty diversity and retention of, 57–58; retention of, 57–58, 138–140

Employer of choice, 48–49

Employment testing, 107–109; advantages of, 108; disadvantages of, 108–109

Equal Employment laws, 68

Equal Pay Act, 68

Equity in compensation, 33–34

Evaluating new hires, 140

External equity in compensation, 34

F

Feild, H. S., 88, 111, 127

Filing discrimination complaints, 73–78; about, 73–74; defense of hiring practices, 74–78; plaintiff's burden of proof, 74–75

Fit Factors, identifying institutional, 22, 26–28

Four-fifths Rule, 76

G

Gallup Organization, The, 137

Gamson, Z. F., 23

Gatewood, R. D., 88, 111, 127

Gender, 99

Gigerenzer, G., 127

Gleser, G., 127

Gmelch, W. H., 25

Greenberg, J., 33

Growth: projecting demand and supply for staff, 39–41; unanticipated hiring needs and PATH, 41–48

Guzzo, R. A., 17

H

Harvey, R. J., 28

Health, 100

Health benefits, 35

Heneman, H. G., 111

Heneman, R. L., 111

Henry, R. A., 8

Higher education: choosing qualified staff in, 3–4; hiring in private industry vs., 4; slow talent flow in, 56–57

Highhouse, S., 17

High-Impact Hiring (Rosse and Levin), 88

Hiring Decision Guide, 127–131; creating, 127, 130; example of, 129;

mance Attributes Matrix, 92–93;
moral-ethical perspectives, 65–66;
performance-based hiring, 64–65,
77–78, 80–81; social context of
hiring laws, 62–64; sources of legal
guidelines, 67–69
Levin, R. A., 8, 24, 56, 57, 77, 88,
99–100, 107, 109, 112, 121, 132,
140–142
LoPresto, R., 111
Lottery hiring, 9

M

Marchese, T. J., 27
Marcus, D. L., 25
Marital status, 99
Marketing job to final candidate,
135–136
Maurer, S. D., 14, 97, 102, 105
McDaniel, M. A., 14, 97, 102, 105
McDonnell-Douglas v. Green, 74
Micham, D. E., 111
Miller, J. L., 47, 121
Mission: defined, 21; determining core
values and Fit Factor from, 27–28;
linking hiring requirements to mis-
sion, 21–22
Monitoring hiring procedures, 81
Montez, J., 25
Moral-ethical perspectives on hiring,
65–66
Morgan, R. B., 54
Motivation, evaluating for potential
employees, 8
Murray, J. P., 21

N

Negligent hiring, 114
Negligent retention, 114
Nelson, C., 14
Nelson, Mike, 16
Noon, S. L., 8

O

On-the-job training vs. knowledge at
time of hire, 28

P

PATH (Planned Alternatives to Hiring), 41–48; continuous hiring,
45–46; questions for developing,
42; redesigning jobs to manage
work, 46–47; replacement planning, 42–43; succession planning,
44–45; temporary staffing, 47–48
Perceived fairness of selection procedures, 90, 92
Performance Attributes Matrix: about,
85–86, 115; accuracy of evaluation
tools, 88–90, 91; advantages of,
121–122; assessments to include in,
87–88; comparison of hiring tools,
91; creating, 85–87; developing
composite attribute ratings, 124–
127; ensuring legality with, 91; hiring from attribute ratings, 126–127;
legality of evaluations in, 92–93;
perceived fairness of selection procedures, 90, 91, 92; practicality of
evaluation tools, 90, 91; sample, 86
Performance foundation, 21–28; cer-
tainty- and uncertainty-based hiring, 23–25; critical attributes list
for applicants, 30–31; developing
Fit Factors, 22, 26–28; identifying
critical performance attributes,
28–30; identifying job outcomes,
22–23; linking hiring to mission,
21–22; relevant Risk Factors, 22,
25–26
Performance-based hiring: avoiding
hiring mistakes with, 131–132;
benefits of, 10; creating composite
attribute ratings for, 124–126;
legality of, 64–65, 77–78, 80–
81; scoring qualifications for job,
122–124; selecting search committee members for, 16; systematic
evaluations and, 121–122; understanding performance needs before
hiring, 5–7. *See also* Decision
making
Personal attention for new hires, 137,
138, 139

Piscataway v. Taxman, 80
Plaintiff: burden of proof on, 74–75; defined, 73
Planned Alternatives to Hiring. *See* PATH
Practicing interviewing techniques, 104
Pregnancy Discrimination Act, 68
Preparing for hiring, 13–36; compensation and, 32–36; defining ideal job candidate, 20–32; search committees' role in, 13–20. *See also* Applicants; Compensation; Performance foundation
Private industry, hiring in, 4
Promotions, succession planning and, 44–45
Protected characteristics: defined, 69–70; legality questions of hiring based on, 78–79
Pursell, E., 101

Q

Qualifications: desirable, 123–124; rating applicant, 122–124; screening applicants by, 120–121; unacceptable, 122–123

R

Race, 99
Ranking applicants, 118
Rating applicants, 118
Realistic job previews, 49–50
Recruiting, 48–56; affirmative action and, 78–80; approaches for attracting applicants, 50–51; building foundation for, 48–50; classified advertising, 51–52; employee referrals, 54–55; Internet job postings, 53–54; realistic job previews, 49–50; search firms and, 55–56
Redesigning jobs to manage work, 46–47
References: checking finalists', 110, 113–115; reference-checking form, 112
Regents of the University of California v. Bakke, 78–79

Relationships: developing with students of diverse backgrounds, 58–59; with new hires, 137–140
Religion, 99
Replacement planning, 42–43
Responses to classified ads, 52
Résumé screening, 94
Retention of staff: after hiring, 140–142; faculty diversity and, 57–58
Ripley, D. E., 111
Risk Factors, 22, 25–26
Ritual hiring: defined, 9; ineffectiveness of, 9–10; performance-based hiring vs., 10; poor decision making and, 120–121
Rosse, J. G., 8, 24, 56, 57, 77, 88, 99–100, 109, 112, 121, 132, 140–142
Russell, J. T., 132

S

Saari, L., 101
Sanches, J. I., 23
Schmidt, F. L., 14, 97, 102, 105
Schmidt, P., 79
Schneider, A., 79
Scoring interviews, 102–103
Screening applicants: developing a screening strategy, 93–96; employment testing and, 107–109; evaluating applicant qualifications, 120–121; identifying attributes needed for job, 85–87; interviews, 96–97; job-related questions during interviews, 97–98; preemployment questions about, 99–100; reference and background checks for finalists, 110–115; scoring interviews, 102–103; tips for interviewing applicants, 103–105; using structured questions, 98, 101–102; verifying critical information, 111–112; work samples, 105–108
Search committees, 13–20; about, 13–14; agreeing on outcomes first, 17–18; checking references, 110,

113–115; composition of, 15–16; cost and effectiveness of, 14; determining role of, 14–15; developing a screening strategy, 93–96; informing applicants of search process, 96; managing decision making of, 17; role of committee chair, 15–16, 18–19; verifying critical information, 111; wrong reasons for hiring, 20–21. *See also* Chair of search committees

Search firms, 55–56

Selection procedures, perceived fairness of, 90, 91, 92

Simon, H. A., 7

Situational Interviewing, 101

Skills, 29

Smith, J. E., 54

Sovereign, K. L., 77

Springer, A. D., 79

Staffing: choosing qualified, 3–4; helping new hires into organization, 135–138; projecting demand and supply for, 39–41; retaining, 138–140; temporary, 47–48

State laws, 67

Statutory law, 67

Stecher, M. D., 121

Stewart, G. L., 23

Structured questions during interviews, 98, 101–102

Succession planning, 44–45

Summary qualifications sheet, 94–95

Systematic information gathering, 7

T

Talent flow, 56

Talent Flow (Levin and Rosse), 138–140

Tasks: creating critical task analysis, 23, 24; evolution of, 23–24; identifying job outcomes, 22–23

Taylor, H. C., 132

Temporary staffing, 47–48

Time: breaking cycle of crisis hiring, 38–39; budgeting interview, 103; hiring and, 37–38; required of search committee members, 16

Title I (Americans with Disabilities Act), 68

Title VII (Civil Rights Act), 68

Todd, P. M., 127

Tort law, 69

Training new hires, 137

Turnover, 139

U

Unacceptable qualifications, 122–123

Uncertainty-based hiring, 23–25

United States v. Hayes International Corporation, 74

V

Van der Vorm, P. T., 21, 27

Vendor relationships with search firms, 55

Vitae, screening, 94

W

Waggaman, J. S., 18, 32

Wanous, J. P., 49

Warm-body hiring, 8–9

Weber v. Kaiser Aluminum, 80

Weekley, J. A., 102

Welcoming new hires, 135–138

Whetzel, D. L., 14, 97, 102, 105

Wiesner, W. H., 102

Wilson, R., 47

Wolverton, M., 25

Z

Zickar, M. J., 107, 121